What people are saying about *Crazy Kingdom*:

"Crazy Kingdom provides a simple, effective approach for changing our thinking from Worldly Living to Kingdom Living. Cameron's approach is both practical and powerful. Our relationship with Christ transitions us from existing to living—surviving to thriving—the way our Father always intended us to live."

-Richard King

Col. Richard King has served twenty-eight years in the US Air Force with a variety of stateside and overseas assignments. Rich has a BS in History and a MS in International Relations. He is a graduate of the Air Command and Staff College, and the Air War College. Rich has served in a wide variety of positions and was a faculty member at both Officer Training School and Squadron Officer School. Rich's latest assignment was as the deputy director for force development for the United States Air Force.

"Cameron has identified what may be the biggest struggle we all face and then provided the solution in a powerful, practical, and personal way. His straightforward message and great examples gave me a clearer mindset along with the inspiration and tools to live a more joyful and effective life in the kingdom. *Crazy Kingdom* is a fantastic book that is going to help us all become the faith-based people we so long to be."

-Lee Ellis

Lee Ellis has a BA in history and an MS in counseling and human development. He is a graduate of the Armed Forces Staff College and the Air War College. He has authored or co-authored four books on leadership and career development. Lee's latest award-winning books are titled *Leading with Honor: Leadership Lessons from the Hanoi Hilton* and *Engage with Honor: Building a Culture of Courageous Accountability.*

"*Crazy Kingdom* is a journey into the truths and expectations of the most important kingdom the world has ever known—the kingdom of God. Cameron's insights and revelation truth in *Crazy Kingdom* will inspire and motivate you to enhance the kingdom of God in your life and community."

-Randy Valimont

Randy Valimont has been the pastor of Griffin First Assembly for twenty-five years, creating seven campuses with a Sunday morning attendance of 5,400. He is a sought-after conference speaker and has spoken in over 75 nations. He is the author of *Betrayed* and *Finding Significance in an Insignificant Place.*

"We live in a truly *Crazy Kingdom*. Up is down; in is out; to hoard is to lose; to give is to gain! Cameron has, in this timely book, opened our eyes as to how this *Crazy Kingdom* operates. Read this book, fill out the journal, and discover how His kingdom works on this earth!"

-Philip Cameron

Philip Cameron is an internationally known speaker. He appears regularly on national television programs. Philip is the author of several books; one, *It's Time for Household Salvation*, has 300,000 copies in print. He has been married for over forty years to his wife, Chrissie. He has four married children and six grandkids.

"The kingdom of God is the rulership and government of God over our lives. If we seek first the kingdom of God, Jesus promises not only heaven but a life of abundance now. Cameron King has written an outstanding book on how to apply the principles that Jesus teaches into our daily living. *Crazy Kingdom* is written in a down-to-earth, easy-to-understand manner intertwined with powerful illustrations which penetrate the reader. Each chapter is a brilliant and witty presentation of some major principles Jesus teaches, and all end with practical applications to an abundant-life mindset, as opposed to the survivor mentality, that is prevalent in our society. We are challenged to put into practice these principles in specific areas of our lives such as "Business," "Family," "Creativity," "Solutions," "Prayer," "Health," and "Financial." This is one of the best books out there on the subject of the kingdom of God. I highly endorse and encourage everyone to read and apply it!!"

-David Garcia

David Garcia is the lead pastor of Grace World Outreach Church in Brooksville, Florida. He is the author of *The Gospel of the Kingdom of God* and *Portrait of a Powerful Last-Day Christian*.

EXPLORING THE MYSTERIES OF KINGDOM LIFE

CAMERON KING

Crazy Kingdom: Exploring the Mysteries of Kingdom Life
Copyright 2018 by Cameron King

All rights reserved. No part of this book may be reproduced, stored in a retrieval system, or transmitted in any form or by any means-electronic, mechanical, photocopy, recording, or otherwise-without prior written permission of the copyright owner.

Unless otherwise noted, all Scripture quotations are taken from the NIV, THE HOLY BIBLE, NEW INTERNATIONAL VERSION®, NIV® Copyright © 1973, 1978, 1984, 2011 by Biblica, Inc.® Used by permission. All rights reserved worldwide.

Scriptures marked KJV are from the King James Version, which is public domain.

Scripture marked DRA is from the Douay-Rheims 1899 American Edition, which is public domain.

Contents

Foreword		7
Instructions		9
Introduction		11
Chapter 1	Survival City	15
Chapter 2	Believe It to See It. Don't See It to Believe It.	23
Chapter 3	To Receive It, Give It Away	27
Chapter 4	To Experience It, Honor Others Who Have It	33
Chapter 5	To Be Respected, Respect the Least Respected	39
Chapter 6	To Be Happy, Mourn First	45
Chapter 7	To Fill Up, Empty Out	51
Chapter 8	To Be Seen, Do It in Secret	57
Chapter 9	To Live It on the Outside, Live It on the Inside	65
Chapter 10	To Keep It, Work It	73
Chapter 11	To Get Everything, Focus on One Thing	81
Chapter 12	To Reach the Many, Invest in the Few	87
Chapter 13	To Go Up, You Must Go Down	93
Chapter 14	To Lead, You Must Serve	99
Chapter 15	To Change Your Direction, Change What You're Looking At	103
Chapter 16	To Gain, You Must Lose	113
Chapter 17	To Be Free, Be a Slave	119
Chapter 18	To Live, You Must Die	125
Chapter 19	To Live Eternally, You Must Die Temporarily	131
Chapter 20	Conclusion	137

Foreword

"Are you ready for God-sized living?" If you are, then *Crazy Kingdom*, by my dear friend, author, pastor, and entrepreneur Cameron King, is for you! First, please allow me to speak about the author and the man. Cameron is a man with a passion for all things Jesus. I have watched him walk faithfully and passionately for Jesus the two decades that I have known him. He is a leader of leaders. God has used him to revitalize churches and ministries in an awesome way. I also have seen him as a husband and father who has led his family, like very few could have done, through tragedy, heartache, and transition and into victory. Cameron is a voice for the nations. I believe that my friend has his finger on the pulse of the church, and I believe that his message must be delivered to the masses.

Are you ready for a new God assignment? Then this book is for you! *Crazy Kingdom* will shift your very concept of what it means to live a life of victory. Cameron King has the unique ability to make truth jump off the page and into the mind of the reader. In this book Cameron will challenge your thinking and dreaming. This book will stir you to realize that with God nothing is impossible. If you follow the steps laid out in this book, you, too, will become a fruitful citizen of a *Crazy Kingdom*. Get ready! You will be stirred and stretched as Cameron shows us that many times, a God plan is the opposite of man's plans and concepts. This book is for every believer, young and old, including the entrepreneur, statesman, minister, and young disciple. It is an amazing handbook for the person desiring to achieve maximum spiritual growth and purpose.

You will learn that there is a massive difference in having a religious or cultural mindset versus a "Kingdom Mindset."

I was reminded as I read *Crazy Kingdom* of what I have believed for so long. That is that God is awakening the next generation of kingdom leaders to arise and stand firm for a spiritual awakening to come to this land. They will be called to lead in all aspects of society. They will also be servants in the church and leaders in the marketplace. Who are they? They will be those that simply realize that they are here for such a time as this. They are the ones who can declare Daniel 7:18, "But the saints of the Highest One will receive the kingdom and possess the kingdom forever, for all ages to come." They will also be the ones who understand that God is raising up "priests and kings" to do the work together. Let us remember as you read this powerful book the words written in Revelation 1:6, "And hath made us kings and priests unto God and his Father; to him be glory and dominion for ever and ever. Amen."

I challenge you to meditate and grow as you read every page. This book is destined to be a classic for next level leadership. Thank you, Cameron, for the awesome ride into the *Crazy Kingdom*. Now let's go live it outside!

—Patrick Schatzline
Evangelist and author, Remnant Ministries International

Instructions

The teaching of this book has the potential to change your life, but there are two tools that you will need to integrate into this material to bring real change into your life. The first is a journal. You will need to prayerfully journal through the questions at the end of each chapter. Write out your answers to the questions so you are able to refer back to them later. This fleshing out of the material in the book within the context of your life is the most important exercise you can complete to leverage this teaching into practical life change. The second tool is a calendar. Your aspirations must have teeth. So write it out, plan it out, and then schedule it. Determine what you are doing and when you're going to do it. May you have good success as you apply the lessons of the *Crazy Kingdom!*

Introduction

I found myself surrounded by a large group of drug dealers who were looking to make an example out of me. Armed with new ax handles from the local hardware store, they were threatening to beat me down in the parking lot of my high school.

A few weeks earlier, one of my classmates had died in a car accident. He was a central figure in the school's not-so-underground drug culture. In my zeal for Christ, but also in the insensitivity of immaturity, I had used this student's death as a platform to proclaim Jesus and the gospel of salvation. "If you were this student, would you be in heaven or hell?" This infuriated his friends—many of whom were gun-carrying drug dealers.

So, in their grief and anger they plotted against me. They had gotten word that I was staying later after school to take an Algebra II test. I left the school to walk to my truck that was neatly parked in an unusually empty student parking area. As I approached my vehicle, four other trucks filled with teens and fellow students suddenly drove up and surrounded my truck on all four sides. I was trapped! The students in the rear of each truck hopped out armed with handles from hammers, axes, and hatchets. I thought my heart would stop.

The ringleader confronted me with fury regarding the things I said about his deceased friend. Enraged with the idea that his friend could be in hell, he swung the ax handle back to hit me in the head. At that very moment, a girl shouted out that their deceased friend "wouldn't want it this way." She also reminded him that the school "has cameras." This sparked a debate of whether they should "kill me now or kill me later?" I was praying silently: kill me later! As the debate wrapped up, the ringleader put the ax handle two inches from my nose and said, "By the end of this week, you're going to be dead." This was really distressing to me because it was already Wednesday, but at least I wasn't going to die that afternoon!

I don't know if they were just attempting to give me the scare of my life or if they meant business. If it was just an attempt to scare me, then they were successful. Either way, I was afraid for my life. I knew they had the potential to be violent. The school was filled with rumors of wrecks by students who claimed these students had run them off the road or had threatened them with guns. This is not what one would expect in a high school filled with upper-middle-class students, but in the center of American prosperity, I was confronted with a number of jarring spiritual truths that solidified my faith.

The first reality I faced was that serving Christ with complete abandonment meant I had to put an end to survival thinking. To follow Christ meant my safety was no longer the predominate concern for my life. I had to crucify the survival instinct. I had to destroy my fear. The culmination of this idea emerged in a confrontation where my life was at stake, and I faced a reality that many Christians in other parts of the world experience daily. Self-preservation is not the priority in God's kingdom. What Paul said is true: I must "daily die" to myself in order to truly live.

The second reality was the understanding of how radically different and antithetical the worldview is between believers and unbelievers. Our paradigms in this situation were in complete contrast to one another. I wanted everyone in the high school to know Christ … be saved … go to heaven. I thought I was doing the most loving thing in the world by using this tragedy as a platform to share the gospel. Yet their paradigm was vastly different. They thought I was tarnishing his legacy and

Introduction

running down his name. In their view, I was the antithesis of love. Not many times since then has this contrast been so concrete, and it usually doesn't involve life or death. The majority of the time it's just the subtle difference between one small decision or another, but the cumulative effect of these little differences in our choices makes for a completely different life.

The third reality is that there are two kingdoms: the kingdom of God and the kingdom of darkness. These kingdoms are at war, and this war is raging everywhere. Sometimes this war is waged in high school parking lots. Other times, the battlefront may arise during a county commissioner meeting or in the lobby of a hotel when traveling for business and an attractive member of the opposite sex walks into the lobby and makes eye contact. Most of the time the war is waged in our head day by day, moment by moment. The conflict is real.

When we accept the kingdom of Christ, we must unlearn every instinct. We must transform our thinking into a lens of understanding that most people will perceive as backward and crazy. The reality is this kingdom, this *Crazy Kingdom*, turns everything that's upside down to right-side up.

In the following chapters, we will delve into these truths by looking directly at the teaching of Jesus. We'll understand the need to execute our survival instinct. Then we'll compare and contrast these different worldviews. We will see that life and thought in the kingdom of God cuts violently through the paradigms and lies of this world. We must choose which kingdom will govern our thoughts, actions, and lives. We will discover what life looks like right-side up from God's perspective and why it's so difficult for us to grab this view.

When you truly give yourself to the kingdom, some people will believe you are crazy. The reality is you're just bringing the *Crazy Kingdom*.

CHAPTER 1

Survival City

> "The time has come," he said. "The kingdom of God has come near. Repent and believe the good news!"
> (Mark 1:15)

The need for survival grips us from all directions. The next bill must be paid. The next meal must be eaten. The next breath must be taken. The drive to survive never stops, even though the realm may differ from person to person. Many around the world are in a daily hunt for food, water, and shelter.

Most people in the Western world have secured such necessities but are still in survival mode. They feel the pressure monthly to pay the mortgage, the growing tab on their credit cards, and the new dance leotard and baseball glove. They have no realistic expectation of homelessness, thirst, or starvation, but they feel like they are just getting by, still living hand-to-mouth or paycheck to paycheck.

Ironically, many of the people who have great achievements or who have amassed piles of money and possessions still worry about losing them. The stock market could crash, they could lose their job, the next real estate bubble could pop, or their company could be cannibalized by the new competition that is leaner, more innovative, smarter, and connects better with the culture. Better stay one step ahead or one cannot survive. The predator could be unleashed at any time, and you better be ready. It is odd seeing the people who have it all but can't enjoy it. They are sitting on the boat dock with a scotch in hand, wondering why they cannot enjoy life. Why do they feel like they are just existing but not living? Where is the joy and the satisfaction in the things they have achieved? They have everything, but can only enjoy it until the new wears off. Then they are back to just taking another breath. They have moved from survival to existing. All of that effort for not much gain. Alive, but not living.

One cannot escape the instinct to survive. It is bred into humanity. It has kept humanity in existence. Humanity has been cursed with the drive to survive and avoid death. Individually one survives by the sweat of one's brow. The human race survives by the pains of childbirth. Cursed with surviving, but never living.

People were created for living, at least initially. Humanity's first setting was in a garden. To be completely honest, a garden does not really excite me. My granny made me work in her garden. I would not consider it fun at all, much less pleasurable. My father owned a small farm in Pelzer, South Carolina. It was his adolescent homestead. When Dad came in my room on Saturday morning and shouted, "Boy, get your blue jeans on," I knew I was not in for a fun day. The nickname my father actually gave our small little farm was Hell. This little farm earned its reputation by having an aversion for rain and being oppressively hot. Dad probably called it that subconsciously, due to the nightmare of his upbringing.

When I first read about a garden, I didn't shout hallelujah. One must keep in mind that the garden was a starting point. It was a home base, so to speak. The garden was God's road sign that said, "Your focus will never be survival. You will only have to focus on living." How does a garden say this? It was the starting point. The garden was as bad as it was ever going to be, and it was paradise! It was all progress from there. The garden must be understood within the context of the command to be fruitful and multiply (Genesis 1:28). There was also the command to subdue and rule over the earth and all that is in it (Genesis 1:29-30). The garden says you'll never fight to survive. The command escorts humanity into God-sized living. You're made in My image, therefore act like Me—create, build, plan, achieve, think, dream, do, rest, and celebrate. In other words, *live!* Humanity was made to live in a perpetual renaissance. The command to subdue the earth is the command to expand the kingdom of God on earth. There is a garden, no need to survive, just live to the fullest. Develop the garden into a city, then turn the city into a kingdom.

Most know that humanity fell. The Devil lied and man died. God told man if you eat of this fruit, then you will die. When I was a little brat in Sunday school, I gave my teachers my own personal commentary on the subject: Adam and Eve ate the fruit, but they did not fall over dead. My conclusion? "God lied."

Yet my conversion would not allow me to take that position any more. So I just accepted that Adam and Eve died spiritually. I went with the safe answer. I think that is true, but that is not the whole story. If death is the absence of life, then anyone who is not living is dead. The fall and the curse that followed it set a new era into motion. A transition took place. Life was no longer about living. Life was now about surviving, and as humanity clung to survival, we existed, but we no longer lived. Unlimited faith, vision, and potential was replaced with fear. Humanity was now dead.

Generations upon generations fearfully existed and survived. These generations found themselves trapped in a cycle of grasping for temporary securities and trite pleasures that resulted in a meager existence, not robust living. Routinely they were left unsatisfied and longing for more.

Now fast forward five thousand years and two cousins pop in on the scene preaching a wild message. John the Baptist and Jesus have a new message: "The kingdom of God is at hand." The same kingdom the Father wanted expanded from the garden is now in reach. John the Baptist and Jesus the Christ are preaching and expecting people to bring that kingdom into their lives, families, and spheres of influence. They're preaching to think and behave like this kingdom is already here.

They were asking us to change our operating systems. I use a certain type of computer that has its own operating system, but if a person desires, this type of computer can run other operating systems too. One computer, two different operating systems. Jesus and John the Baptist were telling us to change our operating system. Their message was repent! Repentance is a change of heart and mind that leads to change in direction. When John and Jesus were asking people to repent, they were telling them to change their operating system. Humanity is operating on one system, but we need to work on another operating system. You are to live in the coming kingdom, and it is getting here so fast it is already within your reach.

To live in this kingdom requires change of heart and mind. One must change one's thinking. Our old operating system is built on the concept of surviving and limited resources. The new operating system is built on life and unlimited resources, power, and creativity. It is a return to garden thinking. It is acting on the image of God within us. Garden thinking and truly living does not sound that hard. This repentance should be no big deal. Yet it is relatively difficult for two reasons—one, no one is living in the garden; and two, the chains of survival instinct bind people tighter than anyone could ever imagine. Yet John and Jesus still call out, "Change your operating system!"

Repentance in the Red and in the Black

Common accounting terminology speaks of being in the red or in the black. When an account is in the red, it is overdrawn. When an account is in the black, it has more money than zero. It has a surplus. Bill Johnson, pastor of Bethel Church in Redding, California, coined the terms "repentance in the red and repentance in the black" in his book *When Heaven Invades Earth*.[1] Most religious folk usually just think of repentance as repentance in the red.

John the Baptist primarily dealt with repentance in the red. Repentance from sin. You know—turn or burn; get the sin out. When someone sins, they go in the red with God. They are overdrawn. As one repents

---

1. Bill Johnson, *When Heaven Invades Earth: A Practical Guide to a Life of Miracles* (Shippensburg, PA: Destiny Image, 2013).

they come back into the black. We understand John's preaching of repentance, but don't understand its link to the kingdom. The drive to sin is, in many ways, linked to the survival curse of humanity. The desire to steal is rooted in survival. I do not have enough; I need yours. Greed and hoarding says, "I might need this later on." Coveting says, "I want what you have because I might need it to survive." Murder says, "I am threatened by you." Breaking the Sabbath says, "I need that extra time to labor or I might not survive." Unbelief says, "Things I can't see don't help me survive." Lying says, "This new set of facts make my survival easier." The list goes on and on. I need your wife, I need to control you, I need more food at this meal, I need more sleep—or I might not survive. The cure for sin is to change our operating system. To move from survival to life. To change the way we think. That is why repentance is accompanied by the message of the kingdom. A new way of life calls for a new operating system.

Jesus added to John's messages. He added "repentance in the black" to the message. There is more to repentance than just changing how we think about sin. Repentance continually modifies our thinking to kingdom thinking. Once we are out of sin, we need to know how to truly live life, raise our families, expand our businesses, enhance our relationships, manage our resources, wield our influence, carry out our ministries, and apply our gifts. The call of Jesus is not only to change our thinking about our sin but to change our thinking about every aspect of life. He calls us to do this violently and forcefully within the context of our own life (Matthew 11:12). This violent and disruptive change in thinking I've dubbed "mind spinning." Jesus invites us to spin our minds around how to really live.

Jesus beckons us to conform our operating system around the reality of absolute life in contrast to mere survival. Jesus calls everyone to live out of the image of God that was placed upon man at the creation. This new operating system returns one's thinking to the pre-fall state of the garden. Without this "repentance in the black," one's thinking will fall back to fearful survival and existence.

You can change your thinking (repentance) and center your mental processes on the eternal kingdom that is within hand's reach and is coming in power on this earth. For the full impact of this kingdom to truly be revealed you must repent, not solely from negative behavior (sin) but from the base desire to just survive. You must change your thinking to how this kingdom affects every area of your life. This change in your belief system will transform your life. *This continual mind spinning is repentance in the black.*

The Counterintuitive Kingdom

Why is it so rare to find people who are truly living? We search in our churches, communities, and institutions but rarely find people who are radically alive. I am sure there are many reasons, but I know one of the reasons is that everything Jesus presents to us about kingdom is counterintuitive. Everything Jesus presents about kingdom living just seems wrong! It feels wrong. It appears illogical. It grinds against our emotions. It unsettles our hearts. It is so unnatural that Jesus tells us that to enter into kingdom thinking requires making radical, violent, disruptive, and forceful decisions (Matthew 11:12). If not, it is so counterintuitive that a simple decision will never carry the force to push through the old web of thinking that rules our minds.

When humanity fell into cursed living, survival became our base perspective. This distorted our view of eternal, everlasting, absolute, and radical life. We see it, but it looks off-kilter. It looks worse than off-kilter. It looks upside down, but not just upside down. It looks inside out. It does not just look inside out. It looks crazy. It feels insane. This does not sound like the path to everlasting life. It looks like the highway to crazy town. If we want to truly live, then we have to be willing to take the step of faith into the gates of the *Crazy Kingdom*.

One cannot fully unravel all the paradoxes that Jesus teaches us; however, we are going to try. You just have to walk out some of these ideas by faith. They work. They bring the kingdom into our life. We

Survival City

don't need to understand every detail of how something works for it to work for us.

I don't really understand how the lights come on when I flip a switch, or why my car moves when I press the gas, or how a big piece of metal floats on the ocean. I just know they work. Many of the ways of the kingdom that we are going to look at, work. I do not always understand how they work, but I know they do. I want you to see the claims that Jesus boldly, and some claim crazily, teaches about the kingdom. I desire for you to step into the paradox. I want to invite you to count the cost, then forcefully, violently, and disruptively move your thinking into the ways of the *Crazy Kingdom*. When you leave the operating system of survival and begin to function on the operating system of absolute life, then it might not seem so crazy after all. It might seem like the world has been set right-side up. Come and let's explore the claims of the *Crazy Kingdom* together.

CHAPTER 2

Believe It to See It. Don't See It to Believe It.

Now faith is confidence in what we hope for and assurance about what we do not see (Hebrews 11:1).

"Have faith in God," Jesus answered. "Truly I tell you, if anyone says to this mountain, 'Go, throw yourself into the sea,' and does not doubt in their heart but believes that what they say will happen, it will be done for them. Therefore I tell you, whatever you ask for in prayer, believe that you have received it, and it will be yours (Mark 11:22-24).

Our natural tendency is that our five senses are king. If we can see it, taste it, touch it, hear it, or smell it, then it is real. This is the framework for life. This is belief. The inbred will to survive demands it. We want proof. If we have proof, then the realm of our survival has known and understood the borders. We can be confident in what resources, dangers, and threats await us.

This view of the world is deceptive. It promises security, but in the end it places limits on true life and never enhances it. This paradigm is also based on the existence of limited resources. It rejects all resources that are not within hands' reach, especially spiritual resources. The atheist says, "I have never seen God; therefore I do not believe, and so He is not a resource I can trust." The doubter says, "I have never seen a major miracle; therefore I don't believe in miracles, so I should never do anything in which I need a miracle." The disappointed Christian says, "I have prayed and not received the answer I wanted; therefore prayer is useless and not helpful for life." This subconscious mindset operates on the premise of a lack of resources. It's trapped in survival foraging.

Yet belief opens our eyes to resources that we have not previously observed—spiritual power, spiritual realities, methods of doing things, human potential, and much more. Seeing these resources and then acting on them actually enforces belief and makes it relevant to life. Unbelief is very limiting. It places a lid on human potential. No matter how great the achievements of mankind without faith, they never reach their full potential.

A faithless state of mind is dead weight on personal growth because when one only believes what is within their personal frame of reference, it makes them, at best, unteachable and, at worst, hopelessly ignorant. Unbelief limits one's horizons by limiting the tools, reference points, and resources that are available to make life work and to make the impossible possible.

We must spin our minds around the reality that belief leads to true life. The kingdom of God is not a resource-based kingdom. It is a creation-based kingdom. If you can think of it, then you can create it. Belief is the conduit that connects you to creative power. This works practically, naturally, and in the spiritual realm. If you can imagine it, then it can be done. There is no cure for cancer, but we can imagine life with one; therefore it will be invented. There are no flying cars, but it is just a matter of time before they start flying off the lot. Every creation, cure, invention, and solution started with an idea and the belief that the idea would become reality.

This limited mindset that has come into our society that says, "There is only one pie and everyone gets a slice of that pie," is a lie based on unbelief that chains the potential of society. The idea of "if I have a big piece, then you have a little piece" creates a small world with small ideas. Yet when one connects with creative power, then they understand they are in a pie factory. Life is not limited to one pie, and society certainly is not limited to one pie. We are pie factories. Connect to creative power and produce pies never imagined before. You can make more pies. There are unlimited resources; we just have to discover where those resources are.

To see it, one must believe it. Faith connects you to spiritual power. Faith releases the floodgates of the power of the kingdom of God into one's life. This power can release miracles. It can open blind eyes, heal the sick, displace evil, raise the dead, find cures, create inventions, produce solutions, raise societies, and enhance culture. If you believe it, you can see it with your own eyes. If you have to see it to believe it, then this need will become the limiting factor in your life.

Business Application

Write out all the services that you would like to see your business offer to the community. Write down what some people would think is impossible for you to accomplish but you think is possible.

Family Application

Write out the possibilities that you see for your family. What do you see as possibilities for your:

- Relationships with your kids?
- Relationship with your spouse?

Do you want to buy a house, travel, retire at a certain age, take family mission trips, or move in your mother-in-law? Just kidding about the mother-in law thing, but truly, the sky is the limit. What do you see ahead of you?

Personal Application

What do you see as the possibilities for your life? Write out every goal and possibility with painstaking detail.

Creative Application

Have you wanted to learn an instrument, garden, or take up painting? Maybe photography is for you? What do you want to create? What do you see?

Solution Application

Is there a problem that bugs you? What skill sets do you have or can acquire to solve that problem? What do you want a solution for? Can you see what can be done? Write out what you are going to do about the problem. Can you invent a process to deal with it? Can you invent something that will solve the problem? What does the solution look like? Now work backward.

Prayer Application

Look at the lists you just made and offer them to the Lord. Meditate on them according to His Word, allowing Him to fill your mind with His fullness, His ideas, His leadings, and His creativity. His plan for your life is based on His limitless grace. As He leads, speak forth the ideas He gives you as you listen to His Holy Spirit.

CHAPTER 3

To Receive It, Give It Away

"Do not judge, and you will not be judged. Do not condemn, and you will not be condemned. Forgive, and you will be forgiven. Give, and it will be given to you. A good measure, pressed down, shaken together and running over, will be poured into your lap. For with the measure you use, it will be measured to you" (Luke 6:37-38).

The drive to survive compels people to hoard everything like chipmunks hoarding nuts in a tree. If one's goal is to survive, then it is logical to store reserves. The laws of mathematics state that if one wants to accumulate more reserves, then they need to add to their reserves, not divide. Therefore, people are going to hoard whatever brings them security. This survival mindset drives people to acquire. If one wants money, then they need to put it in a bank account or stuff it under the mattress. If one wants friendship, when they find a friend or a group of friends, they should not let anyone else in. Protect the reserves. This survival instinct to hoard is rooted in a fear of lack. This fear of lack fuels the fires of hoarding, greed, ruthless ambition, and theft.

A person can survive with that mindset, but they certainly cannot *live*. The kingdom of heaven does not function on survival mode. The kingdom overflows with life. The kingdom overflows with love, creative power, and abundance. If you want more of something, then you must give it away. If one is going to tap into the creative power and the abundance of the unlimited kingdom, then one must act in love. Love always gives. Love is not the priority of survival, but it is the priority of life, a true life link to the kingdom of heaven. When one understands they are operating by kingdom principles, it brings confidence that the resources of the kingdom will be at hand.

Similarly, fruit was at hand for Adam and Eve in the garden. They knew if the resources were not there, then the resources could be created. If it is not there right now, then it will bloom in its season (Psalm 1).

Many understand that God wants us to be generous, and many more understand that the way of love is giving, but few understand how to *receive* kingdom resources. The way to reach one's hand into the kingdom is to create flow.

How do you get started? You initiate! You make the first step. You give. That's why you must forgive to be forgiven (Matthew 6:15). In the kingdom, you make the first step because there is unlimited grace. If you want less of something, then you withhold it. It simply takes you out of flow. God is the Creator, and a river is flowing from His throne. It is flowing into all the kingdom, and when you initiate, then you create flow. Jesus said out of your belly shall flow rivers of living water. Jesus is saying that you become a source of flow.

Jesus also tells us this works in reverse. You don't want to be judged, so you stop the flow of judgment out of you. You don't want to be condemned, so you rein in the condemnation.

If you want to increase something, then you need to start giving it away. Everything you do can become an investment that brings the flow of the kingdom into your life. If one needs more money, then they should give more away. If a person invests their life into a life-giving church, then they will reap a higher quality of life. If someone wants more time, they should give time away in service to others; then they will reap that time back in living longer.

To Receive It, Give It Away

The same is true for you! If you want your business to operate in abundance, creative power, and the blessing of the kingdom, then offer more than is expected to your customers. Offer your customers greater quality than they ever dreamed possible. If you're tired and worn out, then you need to exercise. When you give away energy, then energy will come into your life. If you want friends, then give away friendship and it will return your way. If you want your kids to care for you when you are aged, then invest into your relationships with them now. I am not talking about providing for them or taking them to the movies. I am not even talking about lecturing them about life or giving them platitudes about how to be successful. And I'm certainly not talking about reminding them to wear their seat belt or look both ways before they cross the street. I mean you talk to them, spend time with them, hug and touch them, or whatever it takes to earn a place in their hearts and the right to speak into their lives. Do this continually while they are children, teens, and young adults. Make their new marriage easier rather than being a curse to it. Then one day when you get old, they are going to care for you with compassion. If you don't, then you're going to land in a cheap nursing home on the bad side of town. What you sow is what you reap. You will be provided for, but with no relationship attached to it.

Why? Giving creates flow. Giving gets things moving. You initiate flow for the positive or for the negative. When we are in flow, we are acting out the image of God within us. We are running on the operating system that we were made to run on. The operating system that brings us life. This raises our human potential. This brings creative flow into our lives. This connects us to an invisible kingdom that has no lack and is filled with abundance. This pulls us out of the curse of survival and into real life. Life is about giving. The more you give, the more you live, and in the *Crazy Kingdom* this generous life is rewarded with more resources to be generous.

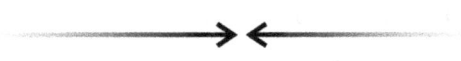

Business Application

Write out all the things that your business can give to others that will not cost you anything financially. Write out all the ways that your business can offer greater quality and service than it has previously offered.

Family Application

Write out which areas your family needs the life of God. Now write out what you can give that will bring the life of God into your family.

Personal Application

Write out everything in which you feel you are lacking. Now consider what you can start giving that corresponds with each thing on that list.

Creative Application

Write out the things that you desire to give yourself that are artistic, create beauty, require craftsmanship, demand skill, and involve problem solving and/or innovation. Now pick the easiest thing on the list and give yourself to it until it is accomplished; then write on your calendar when you are going to start the next easiest thing on your list. Repeat until you have worked up to the most difficult.

Solution Application

Write out a list of things for which you want to provide a solution. Then volunteer or work for a group of people who are presently seeking to solve this problem or a problem similar to it. Keep a journal of the ideas that pop into your head that could help you solve this problem. After three months of journaling, start developing or researching an idea that has popped into your head.

Health Application

Write out what you can do for others that simultaneously makes you healthier. Maybe you can ride bikes with your kids in the neighborhood.

Go to your mother's house and cook a healthy meal together. Join the gym with your spouse and work out together twice a week. Sign up for a 5K race that supports a cause you are passionate about.

Financial Application

Look for two treats that you enjoy weekly, and cut them out and give that money to a cause you are passionate about. It could be as simple as foregoing your five-dollar coffee or maybe brown bagging lunch at the office rather than eating out. Or maybe it could be turning off your cable or satellite.

Prayer Application

Ask God to make you more aware of the needs around you, especially those He wants you to pray over or meet in some way. Keep a record of the needs you see and how they are met.

CHAPTER 4

To Experience It, Honor Others Who Have It

"Anyone who welcomes you welcomes me, and anyone who welcomes me welcomes the one who sent me. Whoever welcomes a prophet as a prophet will receive a prophet's reward, and whoever welcomes a righteous person as a righteous person will receive a righteous person's reward. And if anyone gives even a cup of cold water to one of these little ones who is my disciple, truly I tell you, that person will certainly not lose their reward" (Matthew 10:40-42).

And they took offense at him. But Jesus said to them, "A prophet is not without honor except in his own town and in his own home." And he did not do many miracles there because of their lack of faith (Matthew 13:57-58).

When a person is running the rat race of survival, they are in competition with the ones who are ahead of them. The survival racers always keep track of those who are ahead of them and they always know who is behind them, especially those who are close behind them. Understanding the pecking order of the world is important if one is a survivalist. The survivalist longs to be on top of the food chain. Jealousy is fuel to the survivalist. It provides motivation to keep competing. It is the consolation prize for the first and second runner-up. Jealousy is the salt in the wounds of the defeated. Jealousy is the longing for someone else's experience.

Jesus comes along pointing to the way of the *Crazy Kingdom*. In the *Crazy Kingdom* experience is not hoarded; experiences are multiplied. In the *Crazy Kingdom* if one person experiences something, their experiencing it is the key to someone else experiencing that same reality. The survivalist says, "I am going to push them out of their spot, their experience, because it is only when they are displaced that I can experience what they are experiencing." Experiences are limited.

But in the *Crazy Kingdom,* nothing is limited. One person's success is the key to another's success. One person's experience is the path to someone else experiencing that same reality. Jealousy is the counterfeit of honor. Jesus taught us about how honor works in the kingdom. Jesus said, we had to "welcome a prophet as a prophet." Why must we honor a prophet as a prophet? If they are a prophet, then they are a prophet; what difference does it make about our attitude toward them? The issue is if you want to experience what the prophet experiences, then you must honor him for what he is. You see, the prophet's reward is revelation. If you want revelation from God or from the prophet, then you must honor the prophet. If you want to share in his experience, then you must honor the person who carries that experience. When you honor the man, then you are honoring the price he paid to get to where he is. Honoring the path puts you on the same path. Honoring the person positions you to receive from them, to learn from them, to receive impartation from them, and to acknowledge the work of the Holy Spirit within that person.

Jealousy is honor in reverse. When one is jealous, they desire the experience of another, but the nature of jealousy prevents them from sharing in the experience they desire. Honor is the kingdom path to shared experiences. When Jesus' hometown folks did not honor Him, they could no longer experience His miracles. Miracles don't flow up to the proud, they flow down to the humble.

To Experience It, Honor Others Who Have It

This principle that Jesus taught extends beyond the realm of the prophetic. Jesus qualified that He was teaching a heavenly principle by giving different applications to the same principle. If you welcome a righteous man, then you get the righteous man's reward. What is the righteous man's reward? Righteousness!

If you want to experience what another is experiencing, then don't be jealous of them—honor them! When you honor them, then you share in their experience and you receive from their gift. The path to their experience is a process. To receive from their reward is immediate. When you honor them, their path is highlighted for you. You can follow in their footsteps.

This is not only the key to receive from those above us; it is the key to receive from those under us too. The people who follow our lead have gifts, abilities, and talents. It is only as we acknowledge and honor the gifts they bring to the table that we can receive the full benefit of what they bring.

You must receive a mentor as a mentor to receive a mentor's reward (training). You must receive a pastor as a pastor to receive a pastor's reward (care). You must receive a life coach as a life coach to receive a life coach's reward (perspective and solutions). You must receive an administrative person as an administrative person to receive the organization and order they can offer in your life. The principle holds true in every direction on the ladder.

Most of the time honor is going to be more than simple respect. Honor will require you to give yourself to the person through some means or other. You must pay a personal trainer, life coach, or nutritionist if you are going to receive their reward. Honor may mean you travel to a conference where this person is teaching. Honor may require you to purchase a book they are selling or download material from their website. It may require you to tithe or sow into their ministry. It may require you to purchase their lunch or dinner. Honor demands giving by one means or another. Even if you do something small like a cup of cold water, this will influence what reward you are going to reap from their life. Jesus said even little acts of honor will bring the reward from their life into yours. Remember, if you want to experience the *Crazy Kingdom*, you must honor it.

Business Application

What business is doing better than yours in an area that is important to you? Honor them, speak well of them, and go to them and ask them to teach you what you don't know. If you don't have access to them, have they written any books, do they have a podcast or videos? Watch, listen, and learn. Determine to never be jealous and only speak well of them.

Family Application

If there is a family that is awesome in an area in which you want your own family to excel, then honor them. Have them over for dinner or take them to dinner. Tell them how their example speaks to you and how you want to improve your life. Ask them questions pertaining to how they got where they are.

Personal Application

Identify people who can develop you in the different areas of your life. Who can help you professionally? Make your list. Who can help you spiritually? Relationally? Financially? In your marriage? In your ministry? Make a list. See if you can start developing a relationship with them, and ask them to provide some training, tips, ideas, books that have impacted them, resources they have used. Begin adapting their ideas to your life and see if you can implement them.

Creative Application

Whose work inspires you? Whose work challenges you? Whose work makes you jealous? Who do you feel like you are just a few steps behind? Do something to honor and respect them for their contribution, especially in the area where they have an edge on you. Hang their picture in your office. Write a social media post about their contribution and keep their example in front of you. Celebrate their life and gifts.

Solution Application

Make a pilgrimage to a place that is "getting it done" and making breakthroughs in areas that may be different from yours or in the same field.

Health Application

Interview a person who has made the transition from where you are to where you want to be in your health. Sit down and think through your interview, then journal about the following questions: What did they do that made them successful? What emotional state were they in during this process? What lessons do I need to learn from them?

Financial Application

Go to a conference that can teach you about finances. You know your need. If you are swimming in debt, then you may need to go see Dave Ramsey. If you need more of a faith-based approach to money, then maybe Crown Financial Ministries is for you. If you're wealthy and want to make an impact for the kingdom in a serious way, then maybe you need to go to an event hosted by National Christian Foundation. If you are ready to change the way you think about money maybe you need to go to a Rich Dad, Poor Dad event. The important thing is that you go and sit at the feet of a person who can contribute to your life. Then you can adapt it to your life.

Prayer Application

God is a giver. Ask Him to show you your own heart and give you help in overcoming the enemy within. Jealousy and envy are extremely difficult for us to catch. (Nearly everything eludes us!) But God has the key to our hearts. He can help us in our fight against the evil in our own hearts. As you humble yourself and submit your heart, you honor the work of His Holy Spirit. You put Him first. He will meet you.

CHAPTER 5

To Be Respected, Respect the Least Respected

'Truly I tell you, whatever you did for one of the least of these brothers and sisters of mine, you did for me" (Matthew 25:40).

One of the highest joys of true life is finding mutually beneficial relationships. Yet the survival curse takes one of the greatest joys of life and turns it on its head. This view does not look to mutual benefit within relationships; instead, it looks for individuals to use and manipulate.

Yet Jesus calls us to transform our mind from the pecking order of the barnyard mentality to the reality of God's infinite kingdom. Jesus teaches that you are an avenue for God's unlimited resources to enter the world.[2] Through the perspective of this truth, Jesus calls us to a different way of thinking about how we relate to the humans around us. He calls us to a new way of creating a following. This is not using people to get our way or attempting to find security in the herd of society. This is not climbing one's way to the top to secure one's own resources. Jesus says, "If you have the influence of heaven, then wield this influence, not for the benefit of the strong but for the benefit of the weak."[3]

---

2. See Matthew 7:7, 13:11; Luke 6:38; Ephesians 1:3, 2:6; and James 1:5.
3. See Matthew 19:21; Luke 11:41, 12:33, 14:13, Acts 10:4; Galatians 2:10; and James 1:27.

The weak are crushed by the survival framework built by the world. Jesus proclaims this ironic truth, loud and clear. When one wields their influence to help the weak, then one will gain influence with the strong.[4] One will gain influence with God but also with others with strong influence in society. Plainly Jesus proclaims, "If you respect those who deserve it the least, those who are unimportant, weak, and insignificant, you will gain respect."

Respect in the survival framework says, "Don't mess with them." The world wants respect. Yet the respect the world desires by attempting to be the strong dog or positioning oneself next to the strong dog is given to the one who loves the weak.[5]

This influence and respect, though lusted after, is never secured and certainly is not eternal. Yet love the weak and influence will come your way. This must be supernatural and it certainly is. Who does not respect Mother Teresa? Society respects people who sacrifice for the poor, move to the mission field and preach the gospel to the poor, work with the widow, orphan, the mentally ill, and the handicapped.

Jesus is also directing our attention to an often overlooked fact. There are a whole lot more unimportant people in the world than there are important people. Most of the time the so-called "important people" will never even know you exist. On the other hand, the unimportant will notice you if you just see them, smile, talk to them, or serve them in some way. Many of these people offer respect.

When one does random acts of kindness by helping the unimportant, then the "unimportant" will be open to your endless supply of influence. Hold the door open at the post office for that poor person behind you. Treat the mentally and physically handicapped with respect. Look them in the eyes and shake their hands. Treat that fatherless child with no manners like they are royalty. People will notice and they will respect you. More importantly, God will notice and He will respect you. The

---

4. See Mark 10:24-31 and Luke 18:29-31.
5. See Matthew 5:5 and 5:7.

To Be Respected, Respect the Least Respected

depth of your investment and involvement with the unimportant will be met with reciprocal respect by others.

You will get more respect from these unimportant people than you ever will attempting to impress those not-so-important, important people. Everyone is trying to earn the respect of the important person, so you are just one of many. When you invest in the unimportant with time, energy, and leadership, your influence will snowball. You'll be respected by the compassionate crowd. You will know the school counselors, special education teachers, people who work at the United Way, people who work in social services, community collaboratives, and the list goes on. They will notice your respect and service to the "least of these" and they'll give you their respect and listen to your voice.

There are tons of good-hearted but timid people who want to live like this but are kept in check by the pecking order of life and herd security. They want to live like this, but they don't. However, they'll respect you for doing it. Some will follow suit. The snowball builds as you also gain respect from the families of the unimportant. Your influence has grown because you are now respected by the unimportant, the compassionate crowd, people-pleasers, and families of the unimportant. You are now a leader with influence. This causes the political people to seek you out. They want your vote and the vote of your newfound "voting block." The movers and shakers want you on their side. They don't want to be seen as using people to survive; they want to be seen as compassionate and concerned, and standing next to you will help their image.

All of this flows from God's supernatural blessing and favor on your life. Now you are respected. Now you have influence. Now you are asked to sit at the head of the table. Not because you sought to sit at the head of the table, but because you respected those who were not sitting at the table at all.

The purpose of promotion to the table of influence is to call other movers and shakers to repentance and discovery of the *Crazy Kingdom*. If they do repent, they will spend the influence they have amassed on those who have no influence. Best of all, when one lives like this, God gives them respect. This God-respect might go unnoticed in this life, but it will be openly rewarded in the age to come.[6]

This honoring of all people is intended to be practiced within the church. God intended that the church develop a "culture of honor." This culture of honor is to go from top to bottom within the church creating a place of healing. When individuals who have been used and abused within the survival framework step into the church and they are honored, seen, respected, noticed, served, and valued, healing flows into their hearts. Listen to these two Scriptures.

> The elders who direct the affairs of the church well are worthy of double honor, especially those whose work is preaching and teaching (1 Timothy 5:17).

This speaks of honoring the leaders of the church for their work, service, and guidance. We can say this is honoring the top of the church. But now listen to this Scripture.

> On the contrary, those parts of the body that seem to be weaker are indispensable, and the parts that we think are less honorable we treat with special honor (1 Corinthians 12:22-23a).

This verse speaks of honoring those at the bottom. As these very important, unimportant people are honored, they are healed. First Corinthians 12 speaks of spiritual gifts, but by implication it is teaching a culture of honor. How is it teaching this? The church is to be a place where everyone from top to bottom is respected and honored for what they bring to the table. Everyone has something to contribute. The church is the boot camp for honor and respect in the *Crazy Kingdom*. When we learn the skills of honor and respect in the church, then we

---
6. See Matthew 6:1-4 and Matthew 16:27.

take the *Crazy Kingdom* to the world, especially to the unimportant parts of the world.

Business Application

What can your business do to help, honor, and serve the widow, single mother, elderly person, orphan, or the disadvantaged? Some examples might be taking some of your profits and giving them to a ministry that helps girls who are survivors of human trafficking. Maybe you have leftovers or supplies that can be given to a homeless shelter. Maybe your business does not have the resources to give financially, but maybe you can provide honor. Recognize things like Senior Citizen Day or provide flowers for single mothers.

Family Application

Pick a family project that you are going to do at least once a quarter to serve a group of people the world considers insignificant.

Personal Application

Build a relationship with someone who is poor. The tragedy is not that people are unwilling to help the poor. The tragedy is that people are unwilling to relate to people who are different than they are.

Creative Application

Make a gift, write a song, paint a picture, write a poem, or do something else that does one of three things:

1. Increases awareness of those who are suffering.

2. Moves your heart to serve the unimportant.

3. Allows you to offer a gift to honor ones considered the "least of these."

Solution Application

Find a group that is serving "the least of these." Volunteer some time, but make your main focus recruiting other volunteers or finding them additional donors.

Health Application

Give a gift that will increase the health of someone or help alleviate the suffering of an individual. Offer to pay for some medication, take them a healthy meal, purchase a month at the gym or YMCA. Sponsor a disadvantaged kid at the recreation department by paying for his or her fees and uniforms.

Financial Application

Examine your financial goals. Adjust your goals so they help you serve others. If your goal is retirement at age sixty-five, then make a goal of your retirement to serve at an orphanage in Guatemala for one month out of the year. Or pack your lunch one day a week so you can buy a homeless person's lunch that day. If you want to buy a lake house, then decide you are going to teach five kids each summer how to water ski or have them over to fish once a month. Don't change your financial goals, but adjust them to make sure you are serving the "least of these" as well.

Prayer Application

As you apply serving to your life in a real way, take the time to pray over each and every new relationship God gives you. Speak forth blessing over them, asking God to meet with them and reveal Himself to them.

CHAPTER 6

To Be Happy, Mourn First

Blessed are those who mourn, for they will be comforted (Matthew 5:4).

Most of human behavior revolves around this curse that is related to survival. Yet most people want to escape from this reality. This is the root of our culture's idolatry of fun. This survival curse must be covered, medicated, and escaped from in our lives. In light of it, the world says, "Be happy at all costs." If alcohol makes you happy, then drink to your heart's content. If illicit sex makes you happy, then you should not restrain yourself. There is no need for restraint in anything that makes us happy and rescues us from the rut of survival. Popular culture says jump in with two feet, and whether it's drugs, hanging out with friends, partying, medication, porn, another bad relationship, TV, entertainment, busyness, work, achieving, then so be it. Whatever brings you delight should be pursued.

This race to escape from our human dilemma is futile. We want a deep-seated happiness that radiates from within, not a superficial Band-Aid that only distracts us from reality. Yet the only way to find this kind of happiness is to stop and face the condition we are in and make a change. This is the call of repentance that we hear from John the Baptist and Jesus. The call to face our sin. The call to mourn our condition and then turn from that condition. Humans instinctively run from mourning and repentance. We know we are flawed. The transformation from superficial happiness to a deep joy within must go through the door of mourning. We must stop and face who we really are. Alcoholics Anonymous says it is the point when you realize you are an alcoholic. You are not just having fun; you're a drunk.

True happiness comes when you face the truth, mourn the truth, and deal with the truth. Until you look in the mirror and face the pain and mourn the truth, you will never change. Some need to look in the mirror and say, "I am a bad parent." They need to mourn it and then say, "I am not going to bounce from relationship to relationship any more, trying to fill the void in my life. I am going to focus on my kids." A person needs to go through that same process as they face all behaviors that hinder them. I have made bad decisions, but no more excuses. Face who you are. Do you need to say: I am a liar? I am a slave to the opinions of others? The truth is the most painful thing you will ever face. But the truth is the only thing that will set you free. It is not until you realize that you are a bad parent or an average parent that you can become a great parent, and that brings great joy. It is not until you own your hypocrisy that you can make adjustments, and that coherence of life and thought brings real joy. It is not until you realize that you are not doing well at your job because you are lazy that you can make a real change. The truth hurts. Feel the "un-cushioned" force of the truth. Mourning is the key to change.

The call to mourn also beckons you to dig deeper than your behavior. You also have to face the injustice inflicted upon you in the past. Many times our actions are rooted in the pain of injustice. There might be more to the problem of overeating than what appears on the surface. The problem could be that you are medicating the pain of rejection from a parent who walked out on you. The reason you are looking at porn may be because you are afraid of intimacy, because the last person you shared your heart with rejected you or used that information against you. I am not saying that all bad behavior is rooted in a dysfunctional past, but the call to mourn says, "If it is, then you need to deal with it." If you want to be free, then you have to face the fact—my parents never loved me; the abuse is affecting my behavior; I was taken advantage of.

To Be Happy, Mourn First

The list could go on and on. Facing the past leads to freedom from the past. So how does one cure the pain of injustice afflicted upon them? You can't fix the past, but you can stop running from it. You can face it, then mourn it, and then healing comes. The survival instinct says to run from the pain. It says to run from the darkness of pain. Yet Jesus calls for us to face it, to mourn it, and let the healing process take root. To mourn your loss is the only way to find freedom from the past, and this leads to genuine happiness. Happy are those who mourn.

Mourning is the pathway that helps us to step into a larger world. Mourning things outside of our control places us on a path to greater joy than we could ever imagine. It is a paradox once again. We force ourselves in a direction that is counterintuitive. There are all kinds of injustices that you can mourn—sexual slavery, children with parents in prison, teen pregnancy, misunderstandings that led to further pain that we see in those around us, abuse, and addictions.

When you mourn issues larger than yourself, then the blessings that come into your life are manifold. This mourning releases compassion. This compassion stirs up love in our hearts. This love and compassion connects us to God and motivates us to act positively. Our connection with God and positive action releases the anointing of God's Spirit into our life. This brings a supernatural dimension into our life. We have a supernatural flow of energy, purpose, and miracle-working power. This provides a high to life that can only be understood when one has experienced the connection to a larger purpose.

When one takes this mourning to God through prayer, the Bible calls it *intercession*. The issue that one is mourning becomes catalytic in connecting to God. This connection to God awakens people to the life for which they were created.

We were created to glorify God, know God, and relate with God. When we mourn larger injustices we step into a combination of joy, peace, and purpose that brings an inward satisfaction that awakens us to why we were created. The Bible calls this "joy unspeakable and full of glory"

(1 Peter 1:8b KJV). This holds true until God brings us another cause to mourn. Mourning starts the process that leads to love, compassion, connecting with God, and the anointing. These make us happy. Blessed are those who mourn! Welcome once again to the *Crazy Kingdom*.

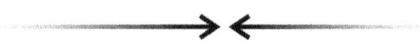

Business Application

Write a list of the things that you have not been willing to face within your business. Write out the consequences if you do not face them. Now go tackle your list.

Family Application

What is the pink elephant in the room that everyone in the family knows is a problem? Call a family meeting and talk about it.

Personal Application

Make a list of the things you have been running from and trying to avoid. This should include emotional problems, unhelpful behaviors, past hurts, forgiveness that you need to give or receive, and dysfunctional relationships that involve you. Pray through this list and ask God to help you deal with these issues. Confess them before God if they are sin. Turn from them. Ask God to heal you in each issue. Then write an action plan to deal with each issue. Every time you face an issue, reward yourself in a healthy way.

Creative Application

Write out the things that you desire to accomplish that are artistic, create beauty, require craftsmanship, demand skill, and involve problem solving and/or innovation. Now pick the easiest thing on the list and begin with it until it's accomplished, then write on your calendar when you are going to start the next easiest thing on your list. Repeat until you have worked up your list to the most difficult.

Solution Application

Is there an issue or cause that grips your heart? What is it? Take five minutes to pray about that issue. Do some research and discover a credible way that you can give and/or volunteer for that cause. Be a part of the solution.

Health Application

Is there a pain you need to see a physician about? Are there some issues in your diet that you need to get under control? Do you need to exercise? Are you digging your grave with your spoon and fork? Do you need to stop smoking? If so, then start learning about the negative effects of these things on your behavior. Find a method that solves the problem and fits within your lifestyle, budget, and personal preference. Work the plan. Make the change.

Financial Application

Are you making decisions in your finances that are going to harm you? Are you behind on your mortgage or car payment? Do you have no plan for retirement? Are there problems you are simply ignoring? What can you do to be proactive? List these problems. Take a moment to panic…I mean mourn. Seek credible resources that will give you sound wisdom on these issues, and start working the plan.

Prayer Application

Prayer changes things. In your time with God, ask Him what areas He wants you to partner with Him in prayer to bring change to the earth. As Father to the fatherless and champion of the weak, He knows everything that happens everywhere. Allow Him to awaken your heart to join with Him in intercession for those who need His help. (Although you may not see the answers to these overarching prayers, He will confirm to you that they are worth the effort. You will grow in your awareness and sense a new kind of closeness to the Lord as well!)

CHAPTER 7

To Fill Up, Empty Out

> Blessed are those who hunger and thirst for
> righteousness, for they will be filled (Matthew 5:6).

If there is any area that survival thinking robs humanity of the most, it could be in the area of emptiness, hunger, and desire. The end game of the survival instinct is continued existence—survival. The natural outgrowth of this principle is apathy. When every threshold has been met for survival, then the goal becomes to maintain. This maintenance mentality soon becomes mindless apathy. Life has now kicked into autopilot. We have our rations, and we can now power down. Apathy and maintenance are not the pathway to true life. We must embrace the path of hunger if we are truly going to live.

Emptiness and hunger do not lead to starvation. Hunger leads to motivation. You are not motivated to eat until you are hungry. If a person is not hungry for excellence, then there is no motivation to improve. If they are not hungry for success, then they will not succeed. If they are not hungry to create, then other things will become a priority. If they are not hungry to solve problems, then they will not solve problems. If a church is not hungry to grow or meet needs or have a community impact, then they will not do that.

We all know the natural order to this. The cycle goes like this: hunger leads to eating; eating leads to being filled. The sensation of being full wanes, which leads to hunger, and the cycle begins again. There are a few variations to this process. When a person eats good things, then their metabolism speeds up, giving them more energy and making them hungry sooner. When a person eats bad things, then their metabolism slows down, giving them less energy and making them fat. The fatter a person gets, the more hungry they become. The brain tells their stomach that they need to consume enough food to provide energy for the body but also enough calories to maintain their fat. Ironically, no matter which path a person chooses, they are going to have an increased appetite. Our bodies illustrate this truth to us every day. To get full, you must be empty.

The same principle is true on multiple levels mentally and spiritually. The nature of what you feed yourself, good or bad, is going to increase your longing for it. If you have been feeding on the bad, then you will desire more of the bad. If you have been eating the good stuff, then your appetite for the good will increase. This is true, but it is not my main point.

When you eat mentally and spiritually, you get hungrier too. Physically, due to the limitation of our stomach to hold food, we have limits. Yet mentally and spiritually, we do not face these limits.

Because of this, the more one eats spiritually, the hungrier they become immediately. This leads to the bizarre state of being hungry and filled at the same time! The hungrier you are for God, the more filled with God you are. Being filled with God makes us even hungrier for Him. The hungrier you are for knowledge, the more filled with knowledge you will be, which intensifies the hunger for more knowledge.

Hunger leads you to that for which you hunger. When you are hungry for answers, then you find answers. Hunger blesses us because it forces us to ask the correct questions. If you are not hungry, there is no reason to seek. If you are not seeking, you will not ask the right questions. The right questions lead you to the right answers. When you are naturally hungry, you ask, "Where can I get food?" It is your emptiness that leads you to fullness. If you are satisfied, then there is no motivation, and without motivation there is no satisfaction.

To Fill Up, Empty Out

You never get full until you get empty. You could paraphrase what Jesus said like this: If one hungers for righteousness, then they are going to ask, "How can I get righteousness?" When you ask the correct question, you will find the correct answer. Jesus was confident in this truth and in the hardwiring of humanity—if one asks the right questions, then they will find the right answers. And in this particular case, Jesus knew that if one asked how they could be righteous, then they would find Him. They would find His grace.

Hunger leads to the right questions. What are the right questions? How do I find what I am looking for? How do I feed my hunger? The right questions improve our life. Outside of random but positive accidents, nothing can be improved in life without us asking how each area can be improved. How can I improve my business? How can I get a promotion? How can I increase the quality of my life? How can I feed all of these kids? How can I afford to take a vacation? You never get there without hunger.

You pair this with the mind and the spirit's ability to never reach capacity, and this leads to a state of being starved and filled simultaneously. When you think about this, you know it to be true. The most knowledgeable people you know are still the hungriest for learning. The most spiritual people you know are still the hungriest spiritually. In the *Crazy Kingdom*, when you're full, you're starving; and when you're starving, you are full.

Business Application

Review your goals: What do you long for your business achieve? What questions do you need to ask to get there? Write these out. Now ask yourself, "Do I need to ask harder questions? Is this what I really desire?"

Family Application

Call a family meeting. Ask everyone in the family what they would like to possess more within the family dynamic. Write down every answer. Then find the root to each answer. For example, if one child says, "I wish Daddy worked less or watched less TV," then know on the base level that they need to connect with their father more. Next, have each family member give priority to each item on the list. Have the family write out a plan, then take action. A word of advice—parents might want to start out with this together first if they have very young children or at least have the right to veto if they have a house full of teens. If not, then you could end up with your top priority being everyone having cable in their own room or something worse. Adapt this idea to be functional for your family.

Personal Application

Write out a list of what you are hungry for in life. See if these things are related. Boil them down to their base issues. For example, no one buys paint for the wall; they purchase beauty. No one wants more money; they want more power or freedom. Boil this list down to what you really want.

Creative Application

What ideas have you wanted to act upon? Write them out and pick the one that has the right balance between functionality and satisfaction.

Solution Application

What problem do you have that you wish someone would solve? Maybe they have. Do some research to see if it has a solution or not. If not, then why not you? Start working on the solution.

Health Application

What do you really want to change about yourself? Is it your appearance? Maybe a lack of energy? Maybe your cholesterol is high. Ask yourself why you have not made a change yet. Now tie your motivation to something really important you like—spending more time with your kids, living to see your grandkids, attracting someone of the opposite sex.

Financial Application

Look at your list from the personal application. Which of these require money? What money can you afford to use to bring about your life goals? If you don't have the money, then what are you going to do to get it? Write out your plan.

Prayer Application

Consider this: God created the emptiness in us so that we would hunger for Him. Just as our bodies need good food to be healthy, our spirit man needs God's Word and presence. The more time we spend with Him, the hungrier we will be for Him. Are you living in this state of holy dissatisfaction? We will never exhaust the depths of God. Enjoy His presence as you hunger after Him and He meets with you daily to continually fill you.

CHAPTER 8

To Be Seen, Do It in Secret

"You are the light of the world. A town built on a hill cannot be hidden. Neither do people light a lamp and put it under a bowl. Instead they put it on its stand, and it gives light to everyone in the house. In the same way, let your light shine before others, that they may see your good deeds and glorify your Father in heaven (Matthew 5:14-16).

"Be careful not to practice your righteousness in front of others to be seen by them. If you do, you will have no reward from your Father in heaven. "So when you give to the needy, do not announce it with trumpets, as the hypocrites do in the synagogues and on the streets, to be honored by others. Truly I tell you, they have received their reward in full. But when you give to the needy, do not let your left hand know what your right hand is doing, so that your giving may be in secret. Then your Father, who sees what is done in secret, will reward you" (Matthew 6:1-4).

Let's start off by reconciling these two Scriptures. One Scripture boldly proclaims, "let your light shine before others, that they may see your good deeds and glorify your Father in heaven." It could be paraphrased as "when people see you doing good works, then they glorify God." The logical conclusion is that the more good works people see, the more they will glorify God. This Scripture certainly encourages public ministry. Your good works serve as public relations for God. The terminology of a "town built on a hill" could easily be paraphrased as a ministry with a platform and influence, a ministry that cannot be hidden.

The second verse tells us plainly, "Be careful not to practice your righteousness in front of others to be seen by them." This Scripture appears to discourage public ministry, opting for secret service instead. Actually, Jesus is building on the same point in the same sermon. One could summarize this passage as saying, "Make sure your motivation for good works is not your own public relations." Love for God and love for others still needs to be the primary motivation, not self-promotion.

Notice that Jesus assumes His followers are going to do good works. Therefore, He instructs His followers that when they do good works, there is no need to announce it. There's no need to attempt to get credit from others for one's good works. God knows and the person served knows, and that is all who really need to know. Jesus was clear. Good works are not the currency for recognition. If you want to be seen by God, then do it in secret. The more secret, the purer the motive, and the more God takes note and the more He rewards.

Even so, because of the previous passage we know that God wants His followers to have a platform. If there is no platform visible or a light on a stand in the dark, then larger groups of people will not see the hand of God at work through His people.

These two Scriptures lay out a spiritual process that occurs in spiritual formation but also cuts across the survivalist mindset. First, a person starts serving privately and/or secretly. As they work privately in service to God, a few things occur:

1. God uses people's service to purify their hearts for more service.
2. Their skills in serving and ministry are developed and refined. Everyone starts at the level of incompetence and grows from that point.

3. God tests their motives and skills. When this process is complete, the Father pulls away the veil that has hidden this secret servant and gives them a platform.

Now everyone in the secret servant's new exalted platform sees a picture of a right person doing rights things, the right way, for the right reasons. The observers get to see a testimony of the heart of the Father—that of a humble servant who loves people.

There are two things about this process we humans don't like, especially if we are still in survival mode. One, this process takes time. Most humans want to shoot to the top as quickly as possible. That might include rising to the top of a corporation, making all-stars in baseball, being first chair in the high school band, or growing that ministry super big and super fast. There is a race to the top. However, most of the people who get to the top the fastest usually don't stay there. I heard one preacher say it like this: "There are no microwaves in heaven, just crockpots." The time of our secret service appears to transform us. That's the point. The survivalist instinct desires to rise to leader of the pack as quickly as we can. Being the top dog ensures our survival.

Second, God built this process into all of humanity. Humans didn't feel the pressure of this before the fall into survivalism. Humanity was going to live forever. You know, "What's the rush?" Yet because humanity fell under the curse of death and the curse of survival, everyone instinctively races against the clock. God is not in a hurry and there is no panic in heaven. No survival instinct there. God takes His time. He is excruciatingly patient. This process has been built into all of creation so you might as well embrace it.

You might as well understand the practical ramifications of this painful process. God graciously allows you to practice in secret. This saves us a lot of embarrassment and pain. God is gracious to us; *this process is a gift*. This process can be summarized in the word *preparation*.

No one sees preparation. A movie might take two hours to watch, but the production of that movie took three years. The reward of secret preparation is the movie itself, much less the success of it. People observe the results of high achievers, and they say, "Boy, they're lucky." They did not see the valedictorian studying for some exam on some lonely Friday night when everyone else was out playing. The Olympian receives the gold on the platform to the cheers of the crowd, but the crowd doesn't see the hours of training, coaching, and practice they endured to get there.

The crowd sees a happy, functional family, while they don't understand the effort it took to create that family dynamic. The crowd was not there before this couple was married, when they were single and they refused to date just any loser who came along, when the selection process looked hopeless, and when the lonely weekends had no end in sight. They don't see all the effort put into communication, working out problems, dealing with differences. Many people say, "They are so lucky to find a spouse like that." Luck had nothing to do with it. If it is seen as a success in public, then it has been practiced long and hard in secret.

If you want to be seen, if you want to have influence, if you want a platform, then you must do it in secret. People are not going to see the light of success and be able to keep it until God says they are ready.

God is not going to pull back the curtain until you are the right person doing the right things, the right way, with the right motive.

In Malcolm Gladwell's book *Outliers: The Story of Success,* he studies people who are hugely successful in life.[7] People who are bigger than life due to their unprecedented success. Naturally, there are countless variables that lead to this. Yet one of the biggest variables is what Gladwell calls the 10,000 hour rule. Research confirms that people at this level of success are very rare. So rare they are labelled *outliers*. To personalize his research, Gladwell presents the examples of professional athletes, musicians like the Beatles, Bill Gates, and many other interesting people. One common denominator can be found among them all—they

---

7. Malcolm Gladwell, *Outliers: The Story of Success* (New York: Back Bay Books, Little, Brown and Company, 2008).

have practiced a minimum of 10,000 hours. When a person has prepared and practiced for 10,000 hours, odds are they are prepared for their once in a lifetime opportunity.

To be seen, you must do it in secret. There are no shortcuts. Shortcuts become lengthy detours. Embrace the process. Practice it with patience. Purify your motives. Develop your skills. Make the pain of the process worth it. This is how you embrace the *Crazy Kingdom*. This is how you will inherit a crazy reward.

Business Application

Have you been taking shortcuts? Have you been cutting corners? What painful processes do you need to embrace in your company or business? Embrace them and work the process.

Family Application

Is there an issue your family needs to face relationally? Is there an issue that is so big you don't feel like you have the energy to tackle it so you have just been ignoring it? If so, bring it into the light, make a personal strategy to work on it, and then have a private conversation with each member of the family whom the issue affects and invite them into the process. If the issue involves children or teens, then inform them that they have been recruited into the process. Make it a matter for family prayer.

Personal Application

List the hard issues you have been avoiding in life or list all the dreams and goals you want to accomplish in life. Write them all down. For each item on the list write out your plan for tackling or accomplishing it. Now look at your paper and say, "If I was God and I wanted to create a person to do this who was the right person doing the right things, the right way, with the right skills, with the right motives, then I would ask:

- What processes do I need to go through to prepare me for this?
- What parts of my heart need to be purified to be prepared for this?
- What skills do I need to develop to be prepared for this?

Now, write out what you think about the answers to those questions, but understand that God is under no obligation to follow the process you just outlined. However, identifying these areas of preparation enables you to start now. Pray about these areas. Pick the easiest skill to develop on your list. Start the preparation process, trusting God to help you and guide you.

Creative Application

Have you started something creative but have not completed it? A painting? A song? A quilt that is half done? An engine that is half rebuilt? A book you started? Maybe the book is finished but has not been edited or sent off to be previewed. Pick up that project and do three things to move the process along.

Solution Application

Have you had ideas to problems you want to solve, but you have not done anything to bring them to fruition? Stay up two hours later than normal or get up two hours earlier than normal and write all your ideas in a notebook. Add all the information that has been floating around in your head about those ideas too. *Put every thought on paper*. Take multiple nights or mornings if you must. Clear your mind. Ask yourself, "What can I do now?" Pick an idea and start moving forward with it. Start working the process.

Health Application

Do you have any health problems that can be solved if you just start practicing a healthy habit or dropping an unhealthy one? While this problem is not going to be fixed overnight, you can begin to deal with it. Set some goals for your physical or mental health. Set a date when you are going to meet each goal. For easy goals, add six months. For moderate goals, add a year. For difficult goals, add two years. For example, you want to lose twenty pounds in six months, and you think that is an easy goal. Add another six months to it. Now your goal is to lose twenty pounds in a year. Figure out how much progress you are going to have to make each month. (In this case, you have to lose 1.67 pounds every month. That is doable. Now add that to your calendar, preferably to your work calendar. Write down your goal to lose 1.67 pounds each week so you will see it every Monday.) What can you do to lose that amount of weight? You decide. There are 10,000 ways to do it. You just have to work the process.

Financial Application

Review your financial goals. Make them if you have not created them yet. What can you start doing right now that will help you with your goals? Do some research. Talk to a financial planner. Understand that it is going to take time to reach your financial goals. Ask yourself the hard questions. Am I willing to do this? Am I capable of doing this? What will be the consequences if I do nothing? If you need to adjust your goals, then do so. Now start the long process a little bit by a little bit.

Prayer Application

Commit your lists to the Lord in prayer. Allow Him to adjust them and ask for His help as you make the changes He leads you to make. Even as you work at all these things, rest in the comfort of His empowerment and grace.

CHAPTER 9

To Live It on the Outside, Live It on the Inside

> "Are you still so dull?" Jesus asked them. "Don't you see that whatever enters the mouth goes into the stomach and then out of the body? But the things that come out of a person's mouth come from the heart, and these defile them. For out of the heart come evil thoughts—murder, adultery, sexual immorality, theft, false testimony, slander. These are what defile a person; but eating with unwashed hands does not defile them" (Matthew 15:16-20).

In a world cursed by an obsession with survival, this paradigm will have natural assumptions. One of the most logical assumptions from this perspective is the concept of "survival of the fittest." This idea was not created out of a science of naturalism. Darwin just finally put words to the dominant thought imprinted upon the human psyche. This evolving idea had burned within human hearts ever since the curse of imminent death had been given to our great-grandparents in the garden.

If the fittest survive, then where one finds themselves in the pecking order is a pressing concern. Yet one common denominator these groups have is that one's place in the pecking order's "success" is determined by external factors. How one moves up the pecking order can be diverse and sophisticated or simple and crude and can depend on culture, geographic need, or even new trends in an ever-evolving society. This ladder climbing can result from sheer force, the guile of manipulation, the fear of witchcraft, political cunning, the weapons at one's command, or the possessions one owns. Every culture defines what the top of the pecking order looks like. This is the definition of success in that culture's external prominence. This external prominence (or failure in it) becomes the label placed upon members of that culture, and when this label is conferred and accepted, it becomes one's identity. Therefore the world's view of identity and success is rooted in *external* realities.

When this worldview is unchallenged within our psyche, then it is natural to come to the same conclusions that modern culture has about success. You are successful if you drive a nice car, live in a big house, have good looking men or women by your side, have lots of money in the bank, and the list goes on. If you have these things, then you are thriving and not just surviving. You are a success! The more success you have, the higher you sit on the totem pole.

The prevalence of such a view still does not protect us from John the Baptist's and Jesus' calls to repentance. This call to live within another kingdom. A call to live in a *Crazy Kingdom*. This mind-spinning, psyche-uprooting repentance calls humanity from the "survival of the fittest" to true life. Our identity and our success do not come from the outside in. They come from the inside out.

In the passage at the beginning of this chapter, Jesus is saying the identity of the "sinner" does not come from the food they eat. What comes from the outside does not determine one's identity or limit one's personal power. The "sinner" label and the behavior of sin comes from the inside out. The message of the gospel is that Jesus provides power to change our internal state, and that new internal state creates a new reality for us on the outside. When one accepts the gospel, they are taking upon themselves a new identity and a new heart. This changes one's reality.

To Live It on the Outside, Live It on the Inside

In light of this, the external indicators that determine one's place in the culture's pecking order does not make one successful. Much of the context of Scripture deals with this reality within the context of dealing with sin. This kingdom principle holds true across the spectrum of ideas and context, but the application is much larger.

The larger application is that your internal reality determines your external reality, not vice versa. One must experience it internally before they can experience it externally. The wisdom of Proverbs states, "For as he thinketh in his heart, so is he" (Proverbs 23:7a KJV). The kingdom does not come from the outside in. The kingdom erupts from the inside out. The atmosphere within you creates the atmosphere around you. You will prosper as your soul prospers (3 John 1:2). In a free society, your internal state will create an external context that will recreate your internal state.[8] The applications are huge. If you are stressed on the inside, you will create circumstances that will create more stress for you. The circumstances do not create stress. They just reveal the stress already present in our hearts. When trying circumstances come, they will be dealt with in an orderly manner (thus recreating the internal state of peace in which we live), or they will be amplified into greater stress (creating a mirror image of our internal state). The same is true for fear. If you are fearful, you will create circumstances that reinforce fear in your life. One of two reactions will occur when truly fearful circumstance arise—you will either start defusing the fear from these circumstances or you will start amplifying the fear.[9] The same is true with lust, greed, pride, and so on.

You will become who you see yourself as being. If you see yourself as a person who has little value, then you will create circumstances

---

8. In societies with no freedom, people are not free to recreate their internal reality. This lack of freedom is an injustice. This injustice steals human potential and is an external force that seeks to halt the potential put in people by God. The leaders of these unjust societies will give an account to God for their sin and oppression. Context is very important. The Bible tells us that nations prosper under the righteous. The righteous give people the freedom to succeed; the unrighteous set up systemic sin that oppresses the natural principles that God has put in place.

9. Naturally, if something traumatic happens, this defusing process will take much longer and may require help to accomplish. But even the willingness to seek help comes from the internal state of the heart.

that reinforce that belief. An example is the young woman who sees herself as cheap and dispensable. She will never be able to say no to "Mr. Wrong." She will never have enough willpower to overcome her identity because it is impossible for her to act outside of it. Mr. Wrong reinforces the belief she has about herself—that she is of little value. She must hear Jesus say, "You're valuable. You're precious. You're significant. You're important. You're so important that I died for you." When she believes this, her internal identity will change and her external reality can also change, and then she can say no to Mr. Wrong and, conversely, yes to Mr. Right. Her identity and her internal reality are everything. Self-control has little relevance to the issue. When she believes this and makes the next step in integrating the teaching of Jesus into her identity, then it becomes easy to say no to Mr. Loser Wrong. Why? He does not confirm the value of her significance. He does not agree with what she *knows* to be true about herself.

This is a two-edged sword that works for good as well as bad. If you have an excellent state internally, then you will create a context that reinforces excellence in your life—a life that now produces excellent products, services, and results. If you see yourself as successful internally, then you'll create a context that lends itself toward success. On the other side, if you see yourself as a failure, you'll continually fail. This is why our identity must be inextricably linked to God. It is only through Him that we can see who we really are. If we see ourselves as pure, then we will start to live a morally pure life. This is why the Bible calls us saints before we act like saints. If you can buy into that identity, then it will change your behavior. Our inner life becomes our reality.

This is true no matter what mistakes you have made, abuse that has been unjustly heaped upon you, ridiculously long history of failure you have had, or location in the pecking order of your society you've been in. To live it on the outside, you must live it on the inside. This is how the *Crazy Kingdom* works.

Business Application

Write out the following: What is the identity of your business? Identify how you, your employees, your community, and your sector define your company's identity. Review your role within your business. What does your identity need to be to be effective in that role? Identify the culture of your employees. What culture do you want displayed by your workforce? How should you cultivate this culture? What internal picture/identity leads to the work environment? Internally how do you need to change your identity as a leader within your business? What must be done to shift the internal identity of your employees about your business? If these internal changes are made, what will some of the tangible expressions of this internal change be, and how can this identity shift the perspective about your business in the community or in your business sector?

Family Application

Write out the following: What labels do the members of your family place upon your family? What labels do you want to enforce and encourage? What labels do you need to work on changing? Start randomly communicating this new identity to your family members. You might start by saying things like, "We have had some problems resolving conflict in the past, but we're developing excellent conflict management skills."

Personal Application

Identify and write down all of the good labels and the bad labels you have given yourself or you have allowed others to give you. Take ten minutes and thank God for all the good things with which you identify. Now what positive labels do you want as replacements for your negative labels? Close your eyes. Ask Jesus to take away your bad labels. Ask Him to communicate the value He has toward you. See yourself living this new identity. Visualize yourself acting out this new label.

Creative Application

What labels have you given yourself that hinder your creativity? Have you limited your views of creativity? If so, then use the same process given above.

Solution Application

What characteristics do problem solvers have? List them and start asking God to cultivate these qualities in your life.

Health Application

Do you have views and ideas that keep you from optimal health? Do you have negative views such as, "I don't enjoy healthy food," "I don't have enough self-control to exercise," or "I will never overcome this cancer"? Ask God to help you with these false beliefs. Then start telling yourself the opposite, but mix them with a good dose of reality and determination. Do it like this: "There are healthy foods I really enjoy, and I am going to find them," "I have the self-control to start exercising, and I am going to cultivate it even more," and "With the help of Jesus and the doctors, I am going to overcome this cancer. I will live and not die. I am going to be a walking miracle."

Financial Application

Ask yourself the hard questions. If you don't like what you find, then ask God to help you and make radical changes. Let me give you some hard questions:

- "Is the reason I am in debt because I am buying things to prove my value to others?"
- "Am I doing all I can to fix my financial problems?"
- "Is the reason I do not enjoy spending or giving because I trust more in money than anything else in life?"
- "Am I carelessly managing my money?"

To Live It on the Outside, Live It on the Inside

Make up your own questions; you know where you need to probe.

Prayer Application

Keep a journal of the words Jesus speaks to you as you apply the truth of your identity in Him. Speak those words over yourself in your quiet time with God and allow them to really sink in.

CHAPTER 10

To Keep It, Work It

> For whoever has will be given more, and they will have an abundance. Whoever does not have, even what they have will be taken from them (Matthew 25:29).

In a life where our most basic subconscious instinct is survival, it is logical to protect the things that are necessary for our survival. Yet the strategy of the hoarders may differ from people to people and culture to culture.

In a materialistic setting the strategy is hoarding. Hoarding provides an imaginary form of protection from an unsure future. Keeping things safe by not using them makes sense. Keeping others from using them is even better. Saving the resources one has ensures they will have them in the future. This protective attitude says my stuff is for me, but it is also larger than this. My talents are for me! My time is for me! My potential is for me! It is all for me! This means every resource is utilized for one's own comfort, protection, and needs. This strategy builds signs around our life that say, "Please don't touch! Keep back! No one needs to use this but me!" This mindset gives the survivalist a false sense of security, but it does offer them some rest from the never-ending work of survival.

Another survival strategy is to only survive moment by moment. These hand-to-mouthers don't take care of anything. If they happen to have extra, they let it rot and spoil. This self-sabotaging keeps them in survival mode, but is also a form of ingratitude that holds in contempt the sacred charge of possessions. These people attempt to rebel against the reality of survival by refusing to take responsibility for their lives. This mindset ensures dependency.

The play-it-safe game plan is another philosophy used by many. These fearful ones seek security. They play it safe on every level of life. Many times these people don't maximize their potential, gifts, and talents because they won't take risks. They don't want to be at the top of the food chain; there's too much pressure to stay there and too large a target on their backs. They just want to hide from predators. This is also a form of ingratitude that neglects the possibilities given to humanity by the Creator.

Once again, Jesus comes to the hordes of survivalists with His mind-spinning new perspective that affirms a new paradox that pushes one off the banks of survival and into the river of life. Jesus does not affirm hoarding or protecting the things that we feel are necessary for survival. Nor does He affirm that we recklessly misuse them. Jesus said in essence, "You use it or you lose it."

The best possible way to protect the necessary and important things in life is not to keep them out of reach but to use them. Use them consistently. Use them thoughtfully. Use them intentionally. Use them for bigger and larger purposes. Our feeble efforts in protecting the things we hold dear only endanger our survival. We have to use it, but we also have to use it well. Jesus taught a great deal on this topic—stewardship.

Another word for stewardship is *management*. If you don't manage it well, then you don't deserve to have it. If one doesn't keep their car clean, then they don't deserve a nicer car. Yet keeping the car in a showroom might protect it from the basic elements, but there is no guarantee the showroom will not burn down or have a tornado plow through it. Everything that one has in life is a tool or an opportunity. These tools and opportunities are to be used to expand our garden and expand God's *Crazy Kingdom*.

God truly does have a sense of humor. He calls us to expand our garden, and the resources we have to expand that garden are metaphorically called our "seed." Our seed can be our energy, possessions, finances, talents, time, gifts, relationships, attitudes, or actions. The best way we protect and multiply our seed is not by hoarding it in some "seed vault" in some dark but dry mountain. The best way to protect your seed is to sow your seed. The best insurance for your seed is to use your seed. Planting one's seed produces more seed. The best way to have seed in the future is to plant the seed you have now.

Yet seed has to be managed with common sense and spiritual insight. One cannot sow seed in the dark of winter and expect a return on it. They must sow their seed in the right season and in the correct "soil." Soil speaks of context. One can sow into the soil of sin, wickedness, and selfishness. They can sow into the soil of small living and minuscule dreams. The other option is to sow into God's *Crazy Kingdom,* which leads to righteousness, peace, and joy (Romans 14:17). The *Crazy Kingdom* flows with true life, big dreams, bigger giving, heart-living, and audacious loving. When you sow into this context, the soil is very fertile.

Anytime you sow, there is a risk. Not every seed comes up, even in good soil. Nevertheless, most seeds come up. Whenever a seed produces fruit, then it is multiplied. Naturally, when one plants a tomato seed, a tomato plant grows from the seed. With the right care, context, and conditions, the plant will be loaded with tomatoes. A large tomato will have more than fifty seeds in it. A fiftyfold return on one's investment is good management. This is just from one tomato!

Most people don't need to worry about how they are going to manage their abundance of resources. The better question is how they are going to manage the little resources. The prophet Zechariah told us, "Who dares despise the day of small things" (Zechariah 4:10a). The problem with managing our small resources is quitting too soon. When one only possesses a little, giving feels like a great sacrifice. Many people start sowing, but they lose patience as they wait for the harvest of their sacrifice. Most people give up trying to improve professionally, paying off debt, saving money, investing, growing spiritually, or losing weight.

They attempt these things. They make small gains, but it takes tons of effort and creates large amounts of discomfort. Most people see their small return and give up because they feel it's not worth the effort. But what they don't understand is these small gains begin to add up over time. One day these small gains reach a tipping point. It takes much time and effort to reach a tipping point, but when one reaches it, everything begins to change. The momentum begins to shift, and gains begin to speed up.

It's like when you played a certain board game based on buying "real estate" spots on the board when you were little. On your first go around the board you landed on a certain spot and you bought it. Then someone landed on your patch of land and they paid you fifteen dollars. It felt like it would take forever to get a set of properties of one color. No, a decade. But then you finally bought all the property that went together. Next you put a house on each of them, then you got four houses, and eventually you put hotels on them. This seemed like it took an eternity, but if you have ever stuck through a whole game you know that when this starts happening the game starts speeding up. Now when an opponent lands on a certain spot, they pay you $250.00. You've worked hard and now have a hotel there, after all! You have now reached a tipping point. All the small progress you made begins to pay off.

The same thing is true in life. You have to fight and scratch to make small gains. If you persist, you reach a tipping point. And when you reach this tipping point, the small gains begin to pay larger dividends.

The more you use your energy, possessions, finances, talents, time, gifts, relationships, attitudes, or actions (the more seed you sow), the better you get at sowing seed. Your skills as a farmer/manager begin to increase. Practice increases your productivity. The greater the productivity, the faster you get to a tipping point. This increase in skill also leads to more advantages and opportunities that accelerate progress even faster.

This process starts a positive cycle in one's life. Small amounts of seed sown in the right context bring small gains. Nevertheless, the

To Keep It, Work It

process of sowing increases one's skill at sowing, which also increases productivity. This adds to an accumulating net of small gains. This increase of skill leads to more advantages and opportunities. Minuscule gains turn into moderate gains. The accumulating net of moderate gains begins to snowball, reaching another tipping point. Now small gains begin to multiply into something bigger and better than anyone would have ever imagined.

This process will prove true in fixing marriages, saving and investing money, paying off debt, growing spiritually, increasing your maximum weight on the bench press, training to run a 5K, growing your small group, or building a ministry. Hopefully people will strive for balance in the seed they sow into differing parts of their lives, and hopefully their lives will hit multiple tipping points at the same time. This creates a tidal wave of synergy that has resulted from sacrificial giving, continually acquiring skills, utilizing advantages, and maximizing opportunities in every area of life, resulting in a life that has reached multiple tipping points for the positive in one's marriage, finances, spiritual life, career, and health all at the same time.

Sadly, if one does not use what one has to make progress, even though progress is slow, then they begin to lose what they have. Marriages fail, bankruptcies are filed, vocations lose meaning, and the body begins to break down. This reality will prove true no matter if people are merely attempting to survive in this brutal world or truly seeking to live in the *Crazy Kingdom*. You are either growing or dying. You are either gaining or losing. You are getting stronger or getting weaker. You are either for Christ or against Him.

Business Application

List what areas of your business need improvement. Write out what seeds you can sow that can produce a harvest in that area of your business. What amount of effort, money, skilled labor, and/or management would it take to reach a tipping point in that area of the business? Is it worth putting that much effort into it? Could it be used somewhere else? Process these questions with a pen and paper.

Family Application

On a sheet of paper draw lines down from the top of the paper to the bottom, dividing the paper into three equal columns. At the top of each column, write the name of each family member you want to impact. This list could include your spouse, children, or grandchildren. Consider what seeds you can sow into this person's life to help them reach their potential in life. One person might need an investment of time. Another might need you to financially sow into their future. Still another might need you to teach them a skill or talent that you possess.

Personal Application

Other than money, write out all the seeds that you have at your disposal that can be sown into whatever area of your life that you desire. Now pick your top three goals in life. What seeds can you sow to help you reach those goals? If you do not have enough of one type of seed to sow into these areas, what are some other seeds you can sow into these areas?

Creative Application

What can you do to sow into your creative side? Can you take a music, art, or fashion class? Maybe your creative side is more practical. Have you thought of getting someone to teach you drafting or the basics of engineering? Maybe you need to try out for a role at your local theater? You could get someone to teach you how to edit video. Maybe you and your spouse need to learn to waltz or fox trot. List your creative desires. Now rank them from easiest to hardest. Now write out how can you sow into these aspects of your life. If you are already busy, then pick the easiest creative desire you have and sow into it. If you have lots of time, maybe you're single or retired, then pick the most difficult desire on your list. Tackle them one by one.

Solution Application

Create a list of all the resources that are at your disposal (your seed). Identify the top ten biggest problems in your life. List them from most urgent to least urgent. If you are short on problems, then you can borrow some from your church, vocation, civic club, work, friends, anywhere at all. Some of these problems may appear to be out of your control. Look at your list of seed. Look at your most urgent problems. What combination of seed can you apply to that problem that will help give you a harvest in solving it? Go through each problem and look at the possible combinations of seed that you can sow into solving these problems. You know your problems better than anyone. You might want to focus your seed on the most urgent problem, but maybe there is nothing you can do about it. If so, then skip to a problem you can solve. Maybe you can knock out problem 3, 4, or 7 on your list. As you solve these problems, you can reap a harvest of peace and greater strength in what you are facing.

Health Application

What seed can you sow into your heath? Do you need to spend more on groceries so you can purchase healthy food that tastes good? Do you need to buy a good multivitamin? Do you need some marriage counseling? Do you need to forgive your sister and give her a call to reconnect? If so, do it.

Financial Application

What can you sow into that will give you more earning power? Can you buy a rental house, stock, or a vending machine? Make plans to purchase something that will give you more earning power in the future.

Prayer Application

There's a tipping point in intercession too. Once you have prayed over a problem, person, or circumstance for an extended period of time, there is a point at which the cup of prayer is filled and God pours it all out.

So do not be weary in well-doing. As you pray, know that none of it is wasted. God will answer. He will never fail to do that. Keep building those hotels! Your reward will be mighty.

CHAPTER 11

To Get Everything, Focus on One Thing

> But seek first his kingdom and his righteousness,
> and all these things will be given to you as well
> (Matthew 6:33).

As we discussed in the first chapter, John the Baptist's message of repentance leads us out of "the red," being dead in our sins, and into "the black." Jesus' message of repentance also calls us out of our sin, but He calls us to more than this. He not only calls us to life, He continually calls us to change our thinking so we can ascend into higher levels of living. Jesus' call does more than just exchange death for life; He shows us how to invest this new life producing abundant life (John 10:10). Yes, He calls us out of deficit, baseline, survival living. Once we get in "the black," He tells us how to really live, and nothing accumulates abundant life faster than *Crazy Kingdom* living. This builds surpluses in the accounts of life. Jesus says that the way to get everything is to focus on one thing—His kingdom.

The world is scattered. Chase this! Pursue that! Jesus is speaking of the power of focus, and He gives us the point of focus too—the kingdom of God. When the kingdom becomes your focus, it creates a gravitational pull on everything that will truly bring you joy. David said it like this, "Take delight in the Lord, and he will give you the desires of your heart" (Psalms 37:4).

Crazy Kingdom

What does it mean to make the kingdom your focus? Your focus is the kingdom when your primary desire is to expand, serve, fight for, represent, speak for, fund, explain, live, and teach the kingdom of God. It is all of this, but the central activity of the kingdom focus is to love the King of the kingdom. This focus on the King and the kingdom means one manages their resources and talents so they can leverage them for the benefit of the kingdom. It means they recruit people into the kingdom, then train these recruits to accomplish the missions of the kingdom and disciple them so they learn the culture of the kingdom. The kingdom is your single focus. Your focus is the kingdom, the kingdom, the kingdom.

This singular focus does not limit life; it actually expands it. This kingdom focus is how you get all the other stuff. In the *Crazy Kingdom*, to get everything you must focus on one thing.

Let me illustrate how this works practically. Jane Doe is working as a nurse at a doctor's office in her hometown. Before she got the job back home, she prayed about what field to go into while she was in high school. After committing her decision to Christ, some months later she had a "moment of clarity" in which she realized she felt compassion for people who were suffering and she enjoyed helping them. During this "moment of clarity," she was also reminded how she was absolutely amazed by God's creation of the human body. In light of these realities as she thought about nursing, she sensed the confirmation of the Holy Spirit to be a nurse.

So off Jane went to college to study nursing. After her freshman year she decided to transfer back to her local technical school to study nursing there. This appeared to be the best decision financially and she loved working in her home church. While at the tech school, she studied hard because she wanted to represent Jesus to her classmates. One of the doctor's offices took note of her due to her positive attitude and work ethic during one of her clinicals, and they hired her immediately after school. Now she's working at the doctor's office. She has a strong work ethic. She is honest and growing in her people skills, all because she wants to glorify Jesus and expand His kingdom. She is zealously kind to her coworkers because she is inviting them to church and she wants to show Jesus to them. Even more than that she has the heart of a servant and goes above and beyond the call of duty. She is producing more than they are paying her for because she sees all of her life as worship to her King. She never stirs up trouble. Office drama is not fun to her, and it would never help her witness. The office manager notices her qualities and interprets them as leadership skills. Jane receives a promotion and receives small but consistent pay increases.

Now let's look at Jane's life from another angle. Jane decided to pay her student loans at an accelerated pace rather than buy what she really wanted—a new car. Nevertheless, she drove the best car she could without acquiring more debt. She decided after her freshman year of college that she was not going to waste her time and money on relationships that were not going anywhere. Six months after getting hired at the doctor's office she met a Christian guy at church. They married in six months, and they didn't have sex until they got married. They had a modest wedding, and their parents helped finically with some of the wedding expenses. Because they managed their resources and their parent's resources so well, they had enough money for a small down payment on a house. Her parents were proud they had not wasted money on the wedding and decided to add to their down payment for their house with the balance of the money they had budgeted for their daughter's wedding.

The young couple started saving small amounts of money and eventually started investing some of the money. They were hoping the investment would allow them to give more to their local church, missions, and charities that helped with humanitarian needs. Their primary focus is the kingdom of God.

Let's leap forward fifteen years. They are not dealing with trust issues, because they know the other person has a track record of sexual purity and in dealing with the opposite sex. They are not loaded with debt. They paid cash for their cars. It took them ten years before they ever acquired a car they really liked, and even then they got it used. Their savings are just now hitting a critical mass, and they are reaping rewards from their investments. They feel a part of something huge, because they have been serving and giving within their local church. There were plenty of times they wondered if they were making a difference, but after fifteen years they can see their impact upon their church. They have developed healthy relationships with other couples and they find satisfaction and security in these close relationships. They sought first the kingdom, and now they have everything else.

When you seek to do God's will first, great benefits come with it.

Business Application

How can you use your business to bring the kingdom of heaven to earth? Start with your relationships with your employees and/or coworkers. How can you bring heaven into the quality of products or services you offer? How can you bring the nature of heaven into your customer service? What can your business do to promote kingdom living with its finances? Process this on paper.

Family Application

List all the areas that you can integrate kingdom-first living into your family. Call a family meeting and decide what you can do to integrate the kingdom more and more into your family. Two examples are:

1. Rather than taking a family vacation, you choose to go on a family mission trip.

2. Cutting down what you would spend on Christmas by half and have each person of the family give the other half to a charity of their choice.

Personal Application

List your priorities in life. Use the Bible or the help of a spiritual leader to evaluate if these should be your priorities in life. Replace the insignificant priorities with kingdom priorities. Now write out how you can integrate the kingdom into all of your life's priorities.

Creative Application

Jesus said, "Let your will be done on earth as it is in heaven." Can you make something, write something, plant something, or draw something that will bring the beauty of heaven to earth? Set a time to create what is in your heart. Ask yourself, "How can this serve others?" Now create what is in your heart. Dedicate your project as worship unto the Lord. Some ideas might include writing a short story for your family, planting a flower garden at a local nursing home, painting a picture that reminds you of some miracle God did for you in times past, recording yourself singing a spontaneous praise song to Jesus, and so on. The list is endless.

Solution Application

Jesus said, "Let your will be done on earth as it is in heaven." What are some problems at home, work, church, an organization in which you volunteer like the PTA, and so on? You know they do not have these problems in heaven. Ask God to give you ideas on how to solve these problems. Your idea could be a process, procedure, invention, introducing a new person to the network or institution you're serving, any number of things. Pray about these problems, ask for solutions, and then tune to flow. Start writing out what you feel like God is giving you about these solutions.

Health Application

Write out the ways that you bring healthy benefits to the kingdom of God. Repent of not seeing your health practices as worship to our Father.

Financial Application

Look at your family budget. Now look at what you can cut so you can increase your kingdom giving. Your first goal is to tithe. If you already tithe, then what can you do to increase your giving by one and a half percent? Go down everything you are spending your money on and see where you can make that a tool to invest in the kingdom. You are probably spending money on a mortgage and cable. Can you have someone over to your house from church and watch a television show that you both enjoy? Are you taking snacks to kids' soccer practice this week? Can you include an invitation to church or a prayer request card for their parents? Are you buying gardening supplies? Can you dedicate the beauty of that garden to the glory of God? When you are buying groceries, can you decide to say encouraging things to two different people while you're at the store? What can you do to make every part of your finances an investment in the kingdom?

Prayer Application

Scripture tells us that if we take every worry, every anxiety, every fear to God and give it to Him, He will keep us in His peace (Philippians 4:6-7). As we do this in prayer, it frees us to focus on the kingdom opportunities in our lives. Many of those opportunities can be applied to prayer. As you meet people daily, you can take their worries and fears to the throne of God and pray for them. People are often quick to allow you to pray for their troubles. Not only will they know you are praying for them, but you will release the Holy Spirit's power over their lives too.

CHAPTER 12

To Reach the Many, Invest in the Few

> Therefore go and make disciples of all nations, baptizing them in the name of the Father and of the Son and of the Holy Spirit, and teaching them to obey everything I have commanded you. And surely I am with you always, to the very end of the age" (Matthew 28:19-20).

> Because we loved you so much, we were delighted to share with you not only the gospel of God but our lives as well (1 Thessalonians 2:8b).

When one is seeking security for their financial investments, the mantra of financial advisors is "diversify." If one invests in many different companies, projects, ideas, and municipalities, then if one company loses value or if one city does not pay their bond holder, then hopefully the others will perform well. You must diversify. This is certainly the best strategy for security and safety.

Many big box stores offer a low-cost strategy. The philosophy of this strategy is to reach as many people as possible by offering the lowest price on common goods. They might not make as much per can of green beans, but they will sell more green beans. The goal is volume. They are attempting to reach the many.

Jesus, John the Baptist, and eventually Paul the Apostle taught us how to invest our lives too, but their investment strategy is done in a different way. These giants do not say to diversify. Jesus, John the Baptist, and Paul leave no room for low-cost living, and they draw us away from making small investments in many people. Jesus taught when one makes a focused investment into a person, church, or organization, then God's *Crazy Kingdom* will begin to spread entirely through that entity.

Just like a little yeast spreads through the whole batch of dough, our investment of the kingdom will spread thoroughly and deeply wherever we make a focused investment. This is why John the Baptist, Jesus, and Paul each had a small group of disciples they were mentoring and training. Why? If you want to reach the many, then you must invest in the few.

The possibilities are so huge for focusing on the small that Jesus even linked the formation of nations, cultures, and ethnic groups to the importance of teaching individuals to obey everything Jesus said and taught. No one today would question that Jesus and Paul had a huge impact on the world. The way they reached the world was through making quality disciples. In the *Crazy Kingdom,* if you want to touch the masses, then deeply touch individuals. You don't diversify; you focus. You don't develop a low-cost strategy; you invest heavily into one person, one church, one cause.

This requires trust and a belief in people, and both of these cut across the grain of a survival culture that says *trust no one*. Jesus again calls us away from our natural instincts into a mind-spinning, perspective-changing repentance that will lead to a more effective and fuller life. *To touch the many, give yourself to the few.*

The applications are many. If you want to shake nations, then shape individuals. If you want to have an effective church, then have a healthy church. If you want to excel at business, then do a few things with quality rather than attempting to do many things poorly. Focus! Focus! Focus!

To Reach the Many, Invest in the Few

The reality of thoroughly reaching the few is infused with power by the undercurrent of a powerful fact. Quality trumps quantity every time, and eventually quality will always lead to quantity. On one hand, one has the perspective that states, "Achieve as much as possible as quickly as possible," while on the other hand Jesus teaches us, "Focus on the few things you can do, and do them well." If you want to reach the masses, then equip, train, mentor, and coach the few. This is the power of the *Crazy Kingdom*.

Business Application

If you are leading a business, write out ways you can make focused investments in smaller areas, then jot down how you are going to invest in these niche areas. It could be in staff development or identifying a specific slice of the market you are going to target. It could be mentoring an employee you feel has high potential. It might be discovering what area of your business is the most profitable and focusing on developing your strengths. It could be pinpointing an area that needs attention because it is weak, so that it becomes developed and can function better.

Family Application

Write out the areas you feel your family needs focus. Most families are far too busy running from soccer to dance to clubs to piano and so on. It might be time to cut back on the activities and focus on the essence of being a family. Maybe you have a child who has not found their strengths. What can you do to help them and help them focus on this newly discovered strength? Do you have a child who is having behavior problems? Maybe it's time to focus on them a bit. Take them to lunch alone. Get them out of school on a day that you are not working and spend the day with them alone. Maybe you need to focus on encouraging your spouse in one area. Maybe you have a child or family member who is on the verge of a real breakthrough in their life. How can you invest in them that will help them with their breakthrough? Journal this.

Personal Application

Look at your whole life. Where can you focus your efforts that will bring you the most satisfaction? Who are the key people you can invest in who will expand your influence through them? Write out your plan. Now work your plan.

Creative Application

Look at your history of creativity or look at the things you have tried to create since reading this book. Where are your strengths? What gives you the most energy? What has gotten the attention of others? Now start focusing on where you have produced the most quality.

Solution Application

Maybe other people are more suited to solve the problems you are passionate about. How can you invest in them in a way that will help them solve the problem you are both concerned about?

Health Application

Who can you help get well and get healthy? Write their names down. Now that you are making efforts to get healthy, don't take the journey alone. Find a person you can teach about what you are learning. Invest in them by motivating them to be your partner. The effect of this can be compounded if you invest in this person in another area as well.

Financial Application

How can you leverage your money, budget, and resources into investing in one thing? It could be that you need to add an art room to your house. Do you need to build a small workshop? Would your investment in people be maximized if money was added to your investment, or would throwing money at the problem bring complications that could take away from your investment? To invest in these people, do you need to pay for training for them? Bring in a consultant? Pay for their coffee once a week? Have them over for dinner? Think about how your money can help you invest in the few.

Prayer Application

Prayer is an investment too. Journal the areas you feel led to pray over regularly. Trace the changes you see over time. When you pray for others you build bridges in the spiritual realm for them. Those bridges help them later in their lives, even though they cannot even see them. Your investment in their future will reap eternal rewards as God moves in their lives.

CHAPTER 13

To Go Up, You Must Go Down

And he said: "Truly I tell you, unless you change and become like little children, you will never enter the kingdom of heaven. Therefore, whoever takes the lowly position of this child is the greatest in the kingdom of heaven (Matthew 18:3-4).

The best mantra of the survival instinct was captured by the rapper John Reuben in his song "Time to Leave":

Taught young, the world's wisdom
Told life's a game, the earth will be your stadium
Be alert, pay attention
(One day) Even your friends will become the competition
Trust no one but do remember this,
never burn any potential bridges
Know who's who, and what they can do for you
And don't feel bad cause' in the end they're gonna do it to you too
Remember life's not fair
In order to maintain,
your gonna have to let your sensitivity be trained
A machine; more than a human being
What you say doesn't always have to be what you mean
Tell them what they want to hear if it's to your benefit
And words beyond closed doors are insignificant
Push yourself, never be satisfied

Crazy Kingdom

*Even if you don't get it,
at least you died knowing you tried*
(The song does have a positive ending.)[10]

In a cursed domain in which one is forced to survive, it makes sense to want to be at the top of the food chain. Why stop at being the boss? Why not be the king? Why not be the emperor? Why not be a god? Dominate! Demand allegiance! Lie! Kill! Destroy! Claw your way to the top! Secure your place at the top!

To be at the top of the food chain is insurance you are not going to get eaten. To be the top guy at the company ensures that no coworker or middle manager is going to outdo you. To rule your homeowner association with an iron fist is the only way to get protection for your assets.

Jesus gives us a different perspective on getting ahead. If you want to be great in the *Crazy Kingdom*, then you must use what I call the model of upward descent. The model of upward descent is the *Crazy Kingdom's* leadership blueprint. It simply operates on the reality that if one aspires to ascend into greatness or into leadership, then one must descend into servanthood and humility. Jesus illustrates this process with the nature of children. Jesus says that in the *Crazy Kingdom* we must become a child. What does it mean to become a child? The applications are manifold, but one thing is certain—it is the opposite of a life cursed with a survival paradigm.

A child is dependent upon their parents. We are dependent on God. A child has not been forced into the cultural mold, therefore there are no limits in their thinking or in their perceived possibilities. We need to think outside the box as well. A child is creative. In the *Crazy Kingdom* we come up with new ideas. A child is a continual learner. We are

---

10. John Reuben, writer, *Time to Leave: Professional Rapper*, Copyright © 2003 24dlb Publishing (ASCAP) Universal Music - Brentwood Benson Publ. (ASCAP) (adm. at CapitolCMGPublishing.com) / 1600 Publishing (ASCAP) All rights reserved. Used by permission.

To Go Up, You Must Go Down

to grow in our curiosity. A child knows how to celebrate. We are to celebrate victories. A child is in touch with their feelings. We are to be in touch with our emotions too. A child will believe what they are told. We are to have faith. A child uses imagination. Our imagination is the springboard for solving problems and artistic expression. A child longs to please their parents. We should yearn to please God. Children tell you what they think; we are to be forthright. Children like to play; we are to make life fun. Children are pure in heart; we are to have pure motives. Children are persistent; we are to keep trying until we get it. The list goes on and on.

Now let's examine why Jesus' model of upward descent is superior to the survival worldview that is illustrated by John Reuben's "Time to Leave" within the corporate world. The model of upward descent's focus is on creative power while the survival worldview is dominated by the concept of limited resources. It assumes that power, resources, money, notoriety, and influence are limited and therefore must be competed for and protected. The *Crazy Kingdom* says these things can be created.

The call to rise through childlike humility is a call to honest entrepreneurship. God does not say, "Climb the mountain of success." He says, "Create your own mountain." Imagine if we started businesses and corporations that were honest, forthright, created fun environments, kept trying until they got it right, wanted to honor God, thought outside the box, had faith in God and in people, were creative and thought of new solutions to old problems, celebrated victories, and were in touch with the emotions and the feelings of their employees and customers and did not run on a paradigm of lack but on the creation of resources.

Now let your imagination run wild, thinking about how the world would be different if this childlike power was unleashed in all of society and our personal lives. Imagine if our governments, institutions, churches, families, organizations, and educational systems tapped into this creative power! We would not need to climb the mountain of success. We would create our own mountains. Imagine how this could revolutionize our parenting, hobbies, health, fitness, and personal fulfillment. The impact of this model would transform every aspect of society from the arts and sports to architecture. From corporate boardrooms forming strategies to discovering new forms of energy to power our society.

The model of upward descent says the world is not ours for the taking; it is ours for the creating. This is how life was intended to be carried out in the garden before man was cursed with survival. This is how life still works within the *Crazy Kingdom*. The greatest threat to truly living is not death; it is survival. The good news is the kingdom is at hand. Why don't you reach out and take it!

Survival Mindset	Crazy Kingdom Childlike Mindset
Depend upon yourself	Depend upon God
Resources are limited	Resources are created
Conformity of thought	Thinking outside the box
Focus on the grind of life	Curiosity compels us to learn
Stuck in a rut	Celebration
Skepticism and doubting	Faith and trust
Static thinking	Dynamic imagination
Pleasing self	Pleasing God
Deceptive and/or unclear	Forthright
Serious	Playful
Moral filth	Purity
Giving up	Persistence

Business Application

Think about your business. Now forget how you would run this place as an adult. How would you run this place if you were a kid? Would there be slides instead of stairs? Would you throw it rather than hand it? When you celebrate, would you play dance music? Look at every angle of your business through the eyes of a child. Write down your thoughts. Star the thoughts that would not cost much cash and implement them on the first Monday of the month and see how your employees respond. Evaluate their benefits or liabilities. Take out what does not work, add in different ideas from your journal, and keep tweaking and implementing your ideas until you start having a culture shift that you like.

Family Application

What are some things you can do that will add some childlike playfulness to your home? What are some things you can celebrate that are not birthdays, anniversaries, or holidays? What are some games you can play? Make sure you make up a new game. Write these ideas down and do one the first Monday night in the month.

Personal Application

Go outside and skip in your backyard. Go out even if it is raining. Then go to your mirror and practice making funny faces. You must laugh at your funny faces.

Creative Application

Take some time to think of what the world needs that has not been invented yet. Maybe a time machine or a coffee mug that keeps your coffee hot down to the last sip. There are no limits in this exercise. Draw a picture of it. Ask yourself this question: "Why would you like to have this?" What is your root desire? Share it with your spouse or friend and get a good laugh. If you think you can make it, then get to work.

Solution Application

Think of something small that has been bugging you around the house or in your car. (This can't be anything structural.) Don't buy anything, but create a makeshift solution that will solve your problem.

Health Application

Walk backward, do cartwheels, play a game that gets your blood pumping, then dance the hokey pokey.

Financial Application

Spend some money on something fun. How about a trip to a theme park or buying the toy you never got when you were little or going to an arcade or riding a go-cart?

Prayer Application

Children don't worry about the future. They trust that their parents have everything under control. Their needs are satisfied and they can depend on them. The same is true with our heavenly Father. Make a point to rest in His love.

CHAPTER 14

To Lead, You Must Serve

> Jesus called them together and said, "You know that the rulers of the Gentiles lord it over them, and their high officials exercise authority over them. Not so with you. Instead, whoever wants to become great among you must be your servant (Matthew 20:25-26).

Leadership objectives within a survival-based operating system say, "Leadership should use their power and resources toward personal survival and prosperity." If one must lead, then one should dominate and control their followers. This secures the position of leadership and multiplies the leader's personal benefits.

This is why the Roman emperors insisted the people deify them. Securing leadership is only one side of the coin. Leadership must be leveraged to ensure personal prosperity. This is how a leader like Kim Jong-un of North Korea could live like a king while his people starved. Ego-centered leadership is leadership fully submitted to the survival curse. The end game is to position it all for the establishment of one's own glory and the security of one's own kingdom.

Jesus, as with all things cursed with the drive to survive, flipped this concept on its head. Jesus called us to repent of our small and selfish view of leadership. Jesus said, "If you are going to lead then you must serve" (Matthew 20:26). This changes everything. Leadership is not gathering and moving people for one's own benefit. It is gathering and moving people for their benefit and the benefit of the *Crazy Kingdom*. If leadership is about servanthood, then it's not about power, control, dominance, and force.

Leadership is about earned and voluntary influence. In the *Crazy Kingdom* every leader is only a potential leader because they are earning the right to lead through servanthood. They gain influence in people's lives and secure their position by banking a unique mix of past success, integrity, and continued servanthood. This builds a surplus of earned right. The new means of leadership is investing in other people's lives. One no longer leads from position, saying, "Follow me because of my title" or from expertise that says, "Follow me because I know more than you." Manipulation and political positioning are taken off the table. Our means of leadership is servanthood.

This is true in every realm of life—personal relationships, family and political affiliations, vocations, and positions within civic organizations. This holds true in any institution, congregation, or organization. The aim is servanthood. The motive for leadership is for the kingdom of God to come in life and in one's dominion. We lead because we are seeking first the kingdom. Follow me! Let's seek and increase this *Crazy Kingdom*!

Unique to the *Crazy Kingdom*, people can choose to follow or not without any bearing on how we treat or respond to them. The goal of servanthood is not to manipulate people. We are servants of the world; whether or not people follow does not change our status or methods. When one's goal is servanthood, being offended if people do not follow is dismantled. This provides liberty to the leader because there is no pressure to produce certain outcomes, except to please the King of the kingdom. This freedom allows us to serve others with no strings attached. Some will follow. Others will not. Yet we love and serve them all the same. This is the way of the *Crazy Kingdom*.

Business Application

Write out your answers to these questions: In what ways can you increase your service to customers, employees, managers, and anyone else? In what ways can you offer more than is expected? What market niche is not being served adequately, and what ways can you customize your service to these people?

Family Application

Write out the unique and diverse ways your family members need to be served. This needs to be more than, "I must continue to run my kids to soccer practice." Look deeper: "How can I help little Johnny develop character?" or "How can I help him overcome his anger problem? How can I serve my spouse emotionally, spiritually, sexually, and physically?"

Personal Application

Take a moment to confess your sin and repent of selfishness. Ask God to give you a heart to serve in everything you do. Pray this prayer every day for a month.

Creative Application

Do you have a creative skill that you can teach others? Maybe you know a lonely person who would like to learn to paint? What about having that new visitor at church over to your house to work on a project together, or take them a loaf of bread that is your secret recipe?

Solution Application

What problem, idea, or plan needs to be developed to solve this issue that is pressing on your heart and mind? Start doing one of two things:

1. In what ways can I serve a person who is already working on this problem? How can I help them reach their goal?

2. If no one is working on the problem, write out a plan to solve this problem, and accomplish the steps in solving it.

Take a moment to ask God to help you serve the world by solving this problem.

Health Application

Understand that to be a servant you need to be at optimal health. When we are at optimal health, we have tons of energy, our mind is sharp, and we are physically able to serve. Look at some of your previous health goals you made in this book. Take a moment to pray over each health goal, asking God for a passion to serve that is fueled by healthy habits.

Financial Application

In what ways can you use your resources to serve others? Maybe you have extra canned goods that you can give to a person in need. Maybe you have a kitchen appliance that you can loan out to a person who needs it. Maybe you need to start tithing; if you tithe, then start supporting a missionary or a parachurch ministry. Maybe you need to teach a friend how to balance a budget. (But remember, if you do balance one, no hypocrisy allowed.)

Prayer Application

Once all your ideas are journaled about serving others, lay them before the Lord. Quietly wait on Him and allow Him to lead and direct you and perhaps give you even more ideas and expand your vision. Just as His resources are limitless, so are the opportunities to serve others.

CHAPTER 15

To Change Your Direction, Change What You're Looking At

> For where your treasure is, there your heart will be also. The eye is the lamp of the body. If your eyes are healthy, your whole body will be full of light. But if your eyes are unhealthy, your whole body will be full of darkness. If then the light within you is darkness, how great is that darkness! No one can serve two masters. Either you will hate the one and love the other, or you will be devoted to the one and despise the other. You cannot serve both God and money (Matthew 6:21-24).

People presently stuck in survival mode are still made in the image of God. This means they desire to escape the survival life and plug into a life of purpose and meaning. They want to flourish. There is a longing in the heart of man to thrive, not survive. Logically, people know this shift in living will require change—internally and externally. As a result, many people desire to make changes in their life. One thing the survival population and kingdom people have in common is they are hungry for change. Survival people want to lose weight, make more money, be fit, and have more sex. Kingdom people desire to stop sinning, grow closer to King Jesus, and be effective in their ministry. Generally, no matter what is on one's "I need to change" list, the masses do not know "how to" change.

When one gets to a point in life where they are hungry for change and growth, that is a really good place. They need to understand that for real change to occur, they must change what they see. Our feet and our emotions follow our focus. Let me illustrate with a shooting example. To accurately fire a gun, one's focus must be on the target, not the trigger.

This principle has a positive and negative aspect. Because of this, many times the people who have the greatest desire for change are the easiest to get sidetracked, discouraged, or misdirected. Why is this the case? It is because of their focus. It does not matter if one loves or hates what their focus is on, they will become their focus. The zealous pursuit of change can cause one to focus too much on the issue they want to change. The focus shifts from the target to the gun. The focus is now on the behavior. Their desire for positive change does not alter the firm reality that states, "One's focus is where one gravitates," and the greater that focus, the greater the gravitational pull toward that reality.

Let's look at an example in the positive. Say your mother gives you a subscription to a landscaping magazine for Christmas. You start stacking those magazines in your bathrooms and on your living room tables. You start flipping through those magazines, and you start reading some of the articles. The next thing you know, you are thinking, "My yard could use some upgrades." You start noticing the garden section in your closest box store. Your buggy begins to gravitate toward that section, and you start making a few small purchases. Now you're making small upgrades. Your yard might not show up in a famous home design magazine, but my point is this: a small shift in your focus created a small shift in your direction.

This is what Jesus is talking about. You cannot focus on survival and kingdom living at the same time. Jesus is speaking of money, and He addresses our survival mentality. If what you focus on is good (in this case the kingdom of God), then your whole body will be good. Picture your whole sphere of influence being invaded by the kingdom of God. If your focus is survival, in Jesus' example the idolatry of money, then your whole sphere of influence will be evil. Your focus will be one or

To Change Your Direction, Change What You're Looking At

the other. Jesus said your focus would be God and kingdom or money and survival. Jesus' principle of focus holds true no matter what the issue—God or sex, God or power, God or pleasure, God or idols. Up until this point, this is really obvious to us, but it also works in the negative. This can really mess up zealous folks. Let me illustrate how this works in the negative.

When I was a teenager I heard a strong message on sexual purity. I did well refraining from sex as a teenager. I was sixteen and I was still a virgin. Not that I was perfect; I had looked at some porn with the boys on the playground. Sinful, but juvenile behavior. Relatively common for an unsaved pagan. At this point in life, I radically turned toward Christ in faith and repentance. I had fallen in love with Jesus so deeply that porn was the least of my concerns. I still loved being in the presence of beautiful women. Jesus saved me. He did not emasculate me. I was on fire for God and wanted to be all that God wanted me to be.

Until one day I heard this message on sexual purity, and I said to myself, "I am going to be the most sexually pure man ever." I put my focus on being super-sexually pure. I made that my goal and made up tons of additional rules to help me out. Do you know what happened? Sexual temptation and sexual urges increased and got more intense. I never gave in or had any major falls, but I was in misery due to all the sexual temptation. And what had I done? I took my focus off Jesus and placed it on my sexuality and sexual purity. Do you know where my feet wanted to run and my emotions wanted to go? They wanted to run toward sex. Why? Your feet will walk toward what you are looking at and focusing on. This is why legalism is ineffective in making one holy. Paul said it like this:

> What shall we say, then? Is the law sinful? Certainly not! Nevertheless, I would not have known what sin was had it not been for the law. For I would not have known what coveting really was if the law had not said, "You shall not covet." But sin, seizing the opportunity afforded by the commandment,

produced in me every kind of coveting. For apart from the law, sin was dead. Once I was alive apart from the law; but when the commandment came, sin sprang to life and I died. I found that the very commandment that was intended to bring life actually brought death. For sin, seizing the opportunity afforded by the commandment, deceived me, and through the commandment put me to death. So then, the law is holy, and the commandment is holy, righteous and good (Romans 7:7-12).

The law draws one's attention to sin, but the law does not give one power over sin. The law says, "Thou shalt not sin." A strong focus on the law places one's focus on the very sin one is trying to escape. When a person's focus is on, "Thou shalt not," even if their motive is good, their focus is still sin. If a person's focus is sin, then their emotions and feet move toward sin even if they do not want to go there.

Yet when one puts their focus on having a powerful relationship with God, or whatever positive outcome one desires, then their feet and emotions move them toward that focus instead. That focus brings life and gives power. When that happens, one starts keeping the standards of the law. The law, in and of itself, is good because it provides boundaries for our relationship with God. Keeping this in mind, the relationship with God is not about the boundaries. *The relationship is about the relationship.* The law shows us when we are out of bounds. When we are out of bounds that hurts the relationship, and because we love the relationship we come back within the boundaries.

The reason the apostle Paul said "the power of sin is the law" (1 Corinthians 15:56b) is because the law is God's standard. If one's focus is the standard and not the God of the standard, then one will lose spiritual empowerment. Life does not flow from the law. Life flows from God. When one puts their focus on Jesus, then their feet and emotions take them toward Him. When you are walking toward Jesus, you will be walking on the highway of holiness by default. This

To Change Your Direction, Change What You're Looking At

is why the writer of Hebrews said, "Let us fix our eyes on Jesus, author and perfecter of our faith" (Hebrews 12:2). Focus on Jesus, and your walk will be perfected. Holiness is the natural byproduct of a God-focused life. The apostle John knew this principle to be true because he wrote this: "we shall be like him, for we shall see him as he is" (1 John 3:2). When we see Jesus, we are like him.

Guilt becomes an issue for zealous people. The zealous hate failure. No matter how much they hate failure, failure is an unavoidable reality. So if failure becomes one's focus, then their feet and emotions will lead them toward failure. Guilt causes one to focus on themselves. Their sin, their mistakes, their rules. Guilt firmly establishes a person's focus on the negative parts of their life. Perpetual guilt consistently focuses one on the wrong things, which perpetually gravitates one toward failure. This progression of failure is a waste of time, energy, and emotion. This misguided zeal leads one away from their target. The way of guilt is ineffective and unproductive.

Name an issue you're facing. You will never improve by solely trying to do better. You will never win by trying not to lose. You will never be for something by being against something else. Ironically, this means perpetual guilt will never led you to a better place. There is no exit ramp on the guilt freeway. This freeway is a circular loop that keeps people in the cycle of failure.

Yet before we participate in guilt, we experience something that can lead to our healing. It is remorse. Remorse can lead to repentance. Remorse acknowledges we have stepped out of bounds, but we are returning to the field of fair play and regaining our focus on the goal. Repentance, in essence, is a change in focus. Moments of remorse and regret must lead us into quick repentance. When they are allowed to sweep one into a guilt cycle, one will be stuck in that cycle until they fix their eyes on something different, and in regard to Christian living that would be Jesus. The apostle Paul teaches us this:

> Therefore, there is now no condemnation for those who are in Christ Jesus, because through Christ

> Jesus the law of the Spirit who gives life has set you free from the law of sin and death. For what the law was powerless to do because it was weakened by the flesh, God did by sending his own Son in the likeness of sinful flesh to be a sin offering. And so he condemned sin in the flesh, in order that the righteous requirement of the law might be fully met in us, who do not live according to the flesh but according to the Spirit (Romans 8: 1-4).

Condemnation is an unhealthy cycle based on guilt. What happens when we are free from condemnation? We meet the righteous requirements of the law. The freedom from guilt gives us freedom to approach God and focus on God rather than ourselves. When we do these things, life and power flow into our lives.

Jesus and Paul both teach this kingdom principle. Both of them focus on ethics, morality, and holiness. Nevertheless, this principle works in all of life. If you focus on getting by in life, you will get by. If you focus on not losing, then you will lose. If you focus on winning, then you will win. If you focus on solutions, then you will find solutions. If you focus on problems, you will continually find problems. If you focus on cooperation, then you will find ways to cooperate.

This is why vision is so important. Vision is what moves you toward something. When an organization sees the vision, they will move toward it. When a team sees the vision, gravity pulls them that way. What you fix your eyes upon, your feet and emotions will gravitate toward. This explains why there is power in positive thinking. Positive focus will lead to positive action. If you want to change direction, then change what you see in your mind, change what you are looking at, and change your focus. This is how change happens in the *Crazy Kingdom*.

To Change Your Direction, Change What You're Looking At

Business Application

Write out your vision for your business. If you already have a mission statement, vision statement, core values, or the like, then look at them. Decide what target is going to be your point of focus, and arrange your life to keep that as your focus. Make a poster and hang it in your office; arrange your office so you can see your point of focus better. Make a craft or piece of art that will remind you of your focus.

Family Application

Call a family meeting. Come to a decision as a family on three goals—short-term, middle-term, and long-term goals. Make sure the whole family is in consensus about these goals. This should not be the time you place your personal crusade on your whole family. Listen to each other. Once you set your goals, make a plan to help your family stay focused on them. Maybe a short-term goal is to vacation in Paris, France, so you decide you're going to look at places you would like to stay on your vacation. You're going to watch a movie, with a setting in Paris, every week until you can make your trip. You'll make croissants and French bread every Friday until you leave for your trip. You're going to subscribe to a Parisian travel blog, and you're going to put a picture of the Eiffel Tower on the door your family uses to come in and out, and it will stay there until your trip. Whatever your goals are, make a plan to keep your whole family focused on them.

Personal Application

Review the goals that you set at the end of chapter one. As you continue to make the goals a point of prayer, begin to visualize yourself as having attained those goals. Close your eyes and build a picture of them in your imagination with great detail. Once you build the picture, focus on it a while and tell the Lord what you see, then journal your picture.

Creative Application

Have you taken up a creative skill since you have started this process? See yourself working on this skill in great detail, with an audience of one person. God is watching and you're preforming for Him. You are painting, building, playing, singing, writing, etc. for Him. See every detail and offer it to Him as worship.

Solution Application

If there is a problem that you have been actively working toward solving, then see the fruit of seeing the problem solved. If you're a scientist and you are working on a cure for AIDS, then imagine African children hugging mothers who would have died. See hospital beds empty instead of full of sick bodies. Visualize what the fruit of your labor is going to look like.

Health Application

Take a moment to see how your life would look if you were at your optimal health. If you are chronically sick, see yourself cured. If you are obese, see yourself running with grandkids. Find pictures that are similar to the scenes you have imagined and do things to keep you focused. Make similar pictures on your screen saver on your computer, print them off and put them in the front of your school notebooks. Hang them up in your cubical or in some place where you will see them daily.

Financial Application

Keep a sticky note on your top check stating, "Do I really need that?" Make a rule that before you buy online, you need to look at a picture of your financial goals. Place pictures of your financial goals where the pictures go in your wallet. Think of everything you can do to help keep yourself focused on your goal.

Prayer Application

Scripture says that God's answers are yes and amen.[11] He seeks our good. Even His laws were made for our protection. Many of your applications have included visualizing good instead of bad to help you maintain a positive focus in life. Philippians 4:8 says, "Finally, brothers and sisters,

---

11. See 2 Corinthians 1:20.

To Change Your Direction, Change What You're Looking At

whatever is true, whatever is noble, whatever is right, whatever is pure, whatever is lovely, whatever is admirable—if anything is excellent or praiseworthy—think about such things." Scripture clearly indicates the worthiness of meditating on good things. Meditate on this passage from God's Word and journal the many things He brings to your mind.

CHAPTER 16

To Gain, You Must Lose

Anyone who loves their life will lose it, while anyone who hates their life in this world will keep it for eternal life (John 12:25).

Even for someone seeking to live all out in the *Crazy Kingdom,* this concept is still hard to swallow. This is one of the most difficult passages of Scripture to believe. It cuts to the core of one's survival instinct with the sharpest of blades. It is contrary to every view the survival mindset has persuaded us to believe. The survival instinct says if you want it, go for it. If you get it, it will make you happy. The more you want, the more you get, the happier you will be. The survivalist believes the easier the life, the better.

Jesus said the only way to gain in life is to lose it. This is a far-reaching principle with tons of applications. It is the essence of Christianity. If one wants to be happy, then they should sacrifice for others. If one wants joy, they need to get out of their comfort zone and give more than others say is wise. If you think something in the world is going to make you happy, then it probably will not.

It is the crux of the problem that the world has with Christianity. The world says the church should be more malleable and thus adjust to contemporary issues and societal evolution. An example of this is the world says the church should just accept the idea that a person can be a homosexual and a Christian at the same time. Just change with the times, but the church cannot change with the times because this principle is at the center of Christianity. Jesus, in His typical mind-spinning fashion, speaks loud and clear to the issue. The reality is, unless a person is willing to give up their identity and their identification with anything the King says "no" to, then they cannot repent. If one can't repent, then one can't be saved.

This is not a sin specific issue. It does not matter what the sin is—homosexuality, adultery, fornication, theft, or lying. Jesus is not saying the repentant person will feel no temptation. They will! Yet do they have enough faith to live in the *Crazy Kingdom*? Do they have the faith to believe if they deny themselves, their body, and their emotional cravings that they can still find life? And not just life—a greater life. A better life! A happier life! Referring again to the illustration of homosexuality, the world says, "It is a part of who they are, and a person cannot be happy without self-expression."

In contrast, Jesus says, "You cannot be happy without self-denial and self-suppression." The *Crazy Kingdom* says self-restraint and self-denial produces an ecosystem that cultivates true happiness.

It is the crucifixion of instinct. It is the absolute contrast of your reality. You believe going west will make you happy. God says going east will make you happy. Who are you going to believe? If you want to be happy, then do the opposite of what you think will make you happy. Ironically, but consistently, if you live for your own happiness, you will be miserable. If you "waste your life" on God and others, then you will be happy. This crucifixion of instinct has thousands of applications. Admitting mistakes and failures will help your marriage, not destroy it. Taking responsibility will not destroy you during times of failure, but it will create ownership that produces positive change. The extra three minutes on the treadmill will not kill you. Telling yourself no to that Internet purchase will not rob you of a quality existence; the peace of mind of having the extra money in the bank will provide a much longer-lasting benefit.

Trying new things and failing at them does not mean you have wasted your time, money, and energy. A lesson learned through failure is a seed sown into the future that is going to bring you a better life. We generally learn more meaningful and lasting lessons from our failures than we do from our successes. Failure due to attempting new things or acting on new ideas works positive things inside us mentally and emotionally. Failures usually occur within the context of doing new things or engaging in activities where there is a risk of failure. Just the discipline of doing this is a positive thing because it develops skill and courage within us and both are needed for a meaningful life. I am not talking about making the same mistake over and over again due to ill-considered repetition. Yet consistent failures within new ventures, ideas, creations, inventions, systems, processes, models, and markets can put you one step closer to a solution. Thomas Edison failed at the light bulb over 3,000 times. When you are going to places no one has ever been before, failure is part of the learning curve. So even in failure you don't lose life, you gain it. That is how things work in the *Crazy Kingdom*.

Business Application

Make a list of the services you are offering and customers you are serving. Could you cut some of these services to help you refocus and provide better service? Could you target one group of customers to super-serve them?

Family Application

Is there an attitude present you could afford to lose? Is there an activity you can cut out? Is there a place you can simplify? Write out the possibilities, then act.

Personal Application

Can you find a day in the next six weeks that you can spend the day in solitude for the purpose of worship, prayer, Scripture reading, listening, and waiting on the Lord? Schedule the day, then pick the place. Waste a day on worshiping God, then take note of the gain.

Creative Application

Of the projects you have been working on, is there one you need to eliminate or table for a while? If so, pack it up in a box and put it in the attic or back of the closet.

Solution Application

Have you come to a standstill in knowing what course of action you need to take next? If so, spend some time in worship and prayer, then ask God to give you solutions and ideas.

Health Application

Is there a place you can serve a person who is not in better health than you? Maybe you could consider visiting a friend in the hospital, visiting a nursing home, taking soup to a sick friend, taking a walk with a friend who is attempting to lose weight. The options are unlimited. Help someone who is struggling with what you are struggling with, then observe how this loss can be a gain for you.

Financial Application

If you are limited on resources, then what else can you cut to free up some cash? Is it time to give up cable? Is it time to downgrade the car? Is it time to cut out that sport or hobby? You decide.

If you have ample resources, then is there something you're not using you need to reemploy or sell? This could be a lake house, a garage full of junk, or a third car. You still want to live a simple life even in the midst of great wealth. Use this extra money to make a memory—go on a vacation, buy gifts for the grandkids, go sky diving. Use your wealth to live life, not rob it from you.

To Gain, You Must Lose

You may need to do the opposite. Maybe you have been so thrifty, frugal, or cheap that it's time to take your family on a cruise or vacation. Pay for your grandchild's tuition at seminary. Go on a mission trip. Use your money for living, not for storing.

Prayer Application

When your day of solitude is done, you will feel strongly centered. Commit to a daily prayer time to maintain this. Carve out a half hour of your day and designate it as His.

CHAPTER 17

To Be Free, Be a Slave

> What then? Shall we sin because we are not under the law but under grace? By no means! Don't you know that when you offer yourselves to someone as obedient slaves, you are slaves of the one you obey—whether you are slaves to sin, which leads to death, or to obedience, which leads to righteousness? But thanks be to God that, though you used to be slaves to sin, you have come to obey from your heart the pattern of teaching that has now claimed your allegiance. You have been set free from sin and have become slaves to righteousness (Romans 6:15-18).

The world tells us that if we are free, then we get to do whatever we want. We have no one telling us what to do. We are our own boss. We get to go and come as we please. Yet if we use this definition of freedom, we see there is no such thing as freedom. Freedom would hinge on two variables. The first variable for true freedom would be to have no responsibilities. Only a person void of all responsibilities would truly be able to go and come as they please. A person might be free to start a business, but once the business opens there will be responsibility; therefore, the person will not be free. Theoretically they would be a slave to the business. Theoretically, one could be free to run a business with no responsibility, but at this point they would not be free to succeed. Therefore, we can see the first variable needed for the world's definition of success is an impossibility in and of itself. To live in a world of irresponsibility limits our access to success, achievement, creativity, and the chance to excel.

The second variable needed for absolute freedom would be unlimited resources. To be able to go wherever you want, whenever you want, however you want requires great resources. It is impossible for a person to possess great resources and have no responsibility. Look at the list of the top ten wealthiest people in the world, and you will notice that they are loaded with responsibility. With resources comes responsibility. The two variables needed to have worldly freedom are impossible to obtain together; therefore, absolute freedom is a myth.

Yet the Bible promises freedom to people. Freedom is not doing whatever you want to do; it is the ability to say "no" to what you don't want to do. This ability to say "no" is only found in the *Crazy Kingdom*. It starts with the choice of which kingdom you will align yourself with. You have a choice.

This also means that freedom is limited. It can only be experienced in smaller measures. God gives you a choice between the kingdom of darkness and survival and the kingdom of God. Here is the reality: whenever you make a free choice regarding what kingdom you are going to live in, you become a slave of that kingdom. So the question you must ask is, *"What kingdom brings you the most freedom?"* It is similar to the metaphor we used earlier. You can be free to choose to start a business, but once you start the business, then you will be a slave (in some measure) to that business. In some measure it will dictate your life rather than you dictating life to it. When you choose the kingdom of darkness, you receive short-term freedom but long-term bondage.

In the kingdom of darkness your options are expanded in terms of sexuality, ethics, and morals. This kingdom gives you more options up front. The downside is that in the kingdom of darkness your "freedoms" become addictions. You become addicted to drugs, sex, porn, lying, power, self-promotion, materialism, gossiping. The list goes on and on. You no longer have normal drives in these areas; you become driven by them. They become the master and you become the slave. This limits your life more and more. The lack of honesty limits your access to healthy relationships and job opportunities that require truthfulness and trust. The addiction to envy and greed limits your enjoyment of your present relationships. The addiction to fame can limit the freedom you have to hold on to your principles.

The kingdom of God works opposite to this. It requires restraint up front. Only have sex with the person to whom you are married. Don't steal. Don't lie. Don't murder or even be angry or bitter for that matter. Don't covet. Worship God. Don't be jealous. Cut out greed. Keep your commitments. Go to church. Serve people. Tithe. Preach the gospel. Speak well of people who don't speak well of you. The moral and ethical demand upon us can be daunting at first. Nevertheless, restraint employs the power God within us. That restraint funnels our potential, gifts, talents, and creativity. This funneling of power actually increases the power in our life.

The restraint of the kingdom of God serves us in a way similar to how the rails on a track serve a train. The rails restrict the direction of the train, but also harness its power. This harnessed and focused power propels the train forward with great power and speed.

The morals, ethics, and responsibilities in the *Crazy Kingdom* don't restrict our life, they give our life power, purpose, and force. Just as putting a nozzle over one end of the garden hose increases the velocity of the water exiting the hose, the initial restrictions we have create focus, thus adding additional force and power to our life. This does not restrict our life, it amplifies it!

This amplification of our human potential, gifts, and talents actually opens many doors for us. The fact we can be trusted opens doors for us too—doors of intimacy, employment, partnerships. Our work ethic opens doors for us. Moral clarity provides focus for creativity. Faithfulness and stability enable us to build upon solid foundations in our life. Restraint in diet leads to freedom in health. Strong moral conviction leads to a sense of identity. Identity leads to confidence in life. Follow-through leads to respect in business and in the workplace. It gives us the freedom to experience prosperity for a larger purpose. Becoming a slave in the *Crazy Kingdom* makes you one of the freest people on planet earth.

Business Application

In what areas do you need to commit yourself? Write them down.

Family Application

What areas of family life are you weakest? Ask God to give you strength in these areas. Now burn a bridge that will demand allegiance to these areas. For example, if you don't engage with your family through conversation and you're always on your phone or iPad instead, then turn off your wifi every night when you get home from work. Get rid of something that makes it easy for you to be weak in a specific area.

Personal Application

In your mind, go to your gravestone. What life characteristics would you want people to say about you on this gravestone? Double-check and see if this is really what you want to become. Now give yourself to these things.

Creative Application

What disciplines do you need to improve on to reach your creative potential? Identify them; practice them every day. Journal about your progress daily.

Solution Application

What project have you started in this book and not finished? Choose the one that is closest to completion and finish it. It does not matter if you must leave at midnight to get supplies. Pull an all-nighter, give a weekend to it, take a private retreat to finish it.

Health Application

Raise the stakes in getting healthy. Do something that will make your efforts extremely committed. Hire a trainer, dietitian, or get an accountability partner.

Financial Application

Limit your options. As Dave Ramsey would say, "Live like no one else so later you can live like no one else." Set your tithe up on direct deposit. Burn that credit card; turn off your cable. Do something radical. If you have plenty of money, then commit it to a purpose that matters to you.

Prayer Application

Spend time seeking God over the areas you see you need deeper commitment. Ask Him for help in each of those areas. Be sure to journal Scriptures He brings to mind in the process.

CHAPTER 18

To Live, You Must Die

> Very truly I tell you, unless a kernel of wheat falls to the ground and dies, it remains only a single seed. But if it dies, it produces many seeds (John 12:24).

The world has no hope in death. Death is the ultimate end. The death of a dream, a loved one, a career, a desire is the end of what brought joy. It is lost forever. Yet in the kingdom of God, there is more power in resurrection than in life itself. And for something to truly come alive, it must die. This principle of the kingdom touches every part of our life. All hope must become hopeless. Only when hope is resurrected does it become a greater hope because it has conquered death. A dream is birthed in seed form, dies, and is buried, then is resurrected in reality. The farmer loses control of what happens to the seed when he puts it in the ground. No matter how skilled the farmer, only God can cause the seed he has sown to bring forth a harvest. The same process is true for us. There comes a point where we steward and manage all that God has given us. Because we are managing God's gifts to us we sow from these gifts, but we also sow into these gifts. These gifts may be a dream, a goal, or a potential relationship. No matter how diligently we manage these gifts, there comes a point when it leaves the control of our hands. At this point we are no longer able to control or manage anything else in the process, but it is at this point that God steps in with resurrection power and brings harvest out of our dead seed.[12]

---

12. See 1 Corinthians 15:36.

The resurrection life is always greater than the previous life. Just as Jesus' resurrected body is better than His normal body, our body will be better after we are resurrected. God lets it die and resurrects it better than before. The life that comes from God can only be hidden so long. Death is the realm that is out of our hands. It is the point that God takes over. For God to take over anything, it must be baptized in death. We lose control, but God takes over.

Water baptism is not just an act of faith for the new disciple, it is an act of faith for God. Water baptism is God asking people when they first become disciples to commit to a life of dying to self.[13] These new disciples may not understand the full range of ramifications such a radical commitment will enact.[14] So God in faith observes our ceremony that illustrates we have died with Christ in salvation, but He also promises that our life from that moment forward will be a continual baptism ceremony.[15] We are going to continually die to self and perpetually baptize our instincts, sinful desires, and survival techniques. For God to take over something it must be baptized in death, and for God to take over our life we must die with Christ. Baptism comes after conversion to illustrate what happened when we were justified, but it comes before sanctification to illustrate the nature of transformation.[16] There is continual growth of the lordship of the King and the *Crazy Kingdom* in our life.

The life of Christ is a life of death. A dead man feels no pride. You can't offend a dead man. A dead man has no opinion. God is trying to kill you because it is only as you die practically in day-to-day life that He can take over practically in day-to-day life. Amazingly, God allows this to be done bit by bit and part by part. We can partner with God's Spirit to kill anger in our life while lust thrives on the other side of our heart. He can be curing spiritual pride on one side of your brain while you are simultaneously bragging about how great you are at work on the other.

---

13. See Romans 6:1-4.
14. See Acts 2:41-42.
15. See Romans 6:5-11.
16. See Romans 5:16-19, 6:1-4, and 6:11-14.

To Live, You Must Die

Perplexingly, God can be working death in you and injecting you with resurrection power at the same time, and He can do it graciously part by part and bit by bit. So surrender to death! The only way to truly live is to die. Paul said, "I die daily" (1 Corinthians 15:31 DRA). Why did he want to die daily? It was only in death that resurrection power could start flowing throughout his being. It would quicken his mortal body.[17] To truly live you must die. Once you're dead, there is no fear of death. When there is no fear of death, you can truly live. That is why people do not start living until they start dying.

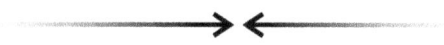

Business Application

Is there an ideal that you need to let go of? A business model, a service in which you are failing, an employee you need to fire, a culture or attitude in the business you need to kill? Journal about this. Make your plan and kill it.

Family Application

Identify the areas in which your desires conflict with your family life. Now kill your desires and actions that cause the conflict. Make this public with your family at a family meeting. What hobby are you stopping? What bad behavior are you eliminating for the good of the family? What selfish pursuit are you stopping for the good of the family?

Personal Application

Is there any attitude that is holding you back? Maybe it is pride, unforgiveness, comparing yourself to others, a victim mindset, blaming other people, fear. It is time to kill these things. Ask the Lord to forgive you of these sins, then ask Him to help you. Now radically move in the opposite way out of your will. If your issue is blaming other people, then determine within yourself that you are going to take personal

---

17. See Romans 8:11 KJV.

responsibility for every issue for the next six weeks, whether it is your fault or not. If your issue is pride, think of all the ways your pride manifests in your life, then do the opposite on purpose, now. If your pride manifests in bragging, then determine you are only going to brag on other people, not even giving a back door to pride. For example, many parents boast about their kids, but they are really communicating, "I am a great parent." Or maybe your pride manifests in arguing. Determine that you are not going to argue with anyone for a month. You are going to hold up the white flag every time. Now get in a small group and confess your issues. Have them hold you accountable and have them pray for you.

Creative Application

Many times creative people have too many projects going. Identify one or two projects that you have started (even projects you have started with this book). You understand they are not the quality you are aiming for. You don't believe they are going to progress much further than their current status. You are no longer excited about them. These projects are completely stalled. If one or two projects meet this criteria, then kill the projects. Trash them and determine you will never work on them again. Write about what you learned from these projects and how these lessons have helped you be more focused in the future. If you feel this way about all your projects, then refocus your efforts, identify the project you feel the best about, and finish it. The discipline of finishing and the momentum of starting and completing a project will lead to more breakthroughs in your life. Just fight your way through this project.

Solution Application

You might need to kill your pride. What ideas are you working on that you need to get help with or perhaps you must give it to another person for further development! Remember you are working on ideas that make the world a better place. It does not matter who gets the credit or who gets paid for it; what matters is that humanity is served. Identify key people you can bring on your team. Discover what incentive will motivate them to join your team. How can you keep them motivated? If you have taken the work as far as you can, then give your work to a more capable leader who can run with it.

Health Application

It is time to prime your health efforts. In your effort to get healthy, what are some things that are not working for you? Rather than quitting, kill what is not working and replace it with something that might work for you. Be sure to write about why these things did not work so you will not make the same mistakes again. For example, you started running but you don't like being alone. Maybe you need to trade running in for a high-impact cardio class. Or you started eating vegetarian, but you really miss meat. Maybe you should move to a high protein diet. Keep your focus on health, but kill what is not working for you.

Financial Application

What are some things, hobbies, events, sinful behaviors that you are spending money on that need to die in your life? The death of these things should save you money. Go public that these things are dead in your life. Put an end to these things with a radical action. Put some serious accountability in place; destroy access to these events. (Sometimes an accountability partner helps with this.) For example, if you are having an affair with a person at work, confess it and get another job. If you struggle with a particular sin, confess it and make a change.

Prayer Application

It truly is amazing the way God works with us. (This is one of the reasons it is so pointless to compare ourselves to others. Everyone is on a different track.) And sometimes it is hard for us to identify areas we need to focus on. This requires a life of continual dying to self and submission to the Lord. Watching our dreams die is a painful process, but as we give Him the reins, He is faithful. Think about your dreams. Pray and journal about them, taking note of any Scripture God gives you in the process.

CHAPTER 19

To Live Eternally, You Must Die Temporarily

The one who believes in me will live, even though they die (John 11:25).

If the goal of the survivalist is survival, then death is the ultimate failure. If death is extinction, then death is ultimate hopelessness. Essentially this struggle is the root of all their vices. Ecclesiastics 3:11b says that God has *"set eternity in the human heart."* This eternal beacon gives humanity the drive to survive. The survivalist mindset is the natural byproduct of imminent death. Death is the byproduct of sin and the curse. God never intended that survival or death would be central to the human equation. Humanity was not created for existence, survival, or death. Humanity was created for eternal pleasure, but this was exchanged for a bloody fight for mere existence so we could have a more intimate knowledge of good and evil.[18]

For the sake of clarification, existence and life are different. People will exist eternally in hell, but life can only be experienced with God. God never designed humanity to exist; He designed them to live. Therefore He brought the *Crazy Kingdom* to give us eternal life. Jesus did not bring the *Crazy Kingdom* to earth so we can exist on earth and finally live in heaven when we die. Eternal life starts now! Eternal life starts here! When we implement the *Crazy Kingdom* into our worldview,

---

18. See Genesis 2:17 and 3:6-7.

Crazy Kingdom

habits, actions, and thoughts in this life, then we start the practice of eternal living now.

Nevertheless, the lingering problem doesn't go away. Everyone will still die physically. When Jesus came to earth bringing His *Crazy Kingdom*, fixing death was the top item on his agenda. Jesus was and is the solution to death because He is the embodiment of resurrection power.[19]

Jesus came to establish a two-step plan. Step one was to provide us with access to the Father, both in life and after death. Access to the Father initiates true life. Giving us access to the Father turned Jesus' death into a birth. The moment we die as a believer, we step into heaven. The apostle Paul said it like this, "I…would prefer to be away from the body and at home with the Lord" (2 Corinthians 5:8).[20] This is an important application. When one fully understands that eternal life starts now, then one understands they continue to carry momentum into the next phase of life.

The Bible is clear that we will rule and reign with Him in eternity. We learn to rule and reign now, through hands-on training. How well we do here determines our reward there.[21] Eternal rewards are bestowed based on the pursuit of our dreams and potential, opportunities, gifts, talents, abilities, and vision within our own dominion now.[22] We bring the rule of the *Crazy Kingdom* to our circles of influence. There are many ways to bring the rule of God to our realm, but one of the primary ways is by applying this upside-down, inside-out, crazy teaching of Jesus to every aspect of our own lives. This will determine our reward and what we rule. Every decision we make in this life for the positive or negative will carry positive or negative momentum into eternity, so implementing the *Crazy Kingdom* is not solely for this life. It's for eternity. As we implement the *Crazy Kingdom* now, we prepare for our role in eternity. It is ruling-and-reigning training. Fortunately the joy and pleasure of

---

19. See John 11:25.
20. Also, see 2 Corinthians 5:1-2.
21. See 1 Corinthians 3:11-15.
22. See Matthew 25:14-30 and Luke 19:16-17.

To Live Eternally, You Must Die Temporarily

the *Crazy Kingdom* starts now. Developing the life God has given us and discovering the potential that is buried in that life is of greater consequence than we can ever imagine.

Remember, Jesus had a two-step plan in dealing with death. Step one was giving us access to the Father. Jesus' step two is bodily resurrection. Bodily, humans still die. The gospel of the life, death, and resurrection of Jesus brings total salvation. Total salvation includes a new and upgraded body. Our old body is sown like a seed in the ground, reaping a great return on our investment.[23] Our salvation will be totally complete—spirit, soul, and body.

Most of the principles of the *Crazy Kingdom* require action on our part. Leaving life to fate is not one of Jesus' concepts. We are learning the way to set the world right-side up. Faith is not passively believing God holds the future. That line of thinking results in a do-nothing lifestyle. Faith is acting on the Word of God to establish the kingdom in one's circle of influence. Vision is seeing the possibilities that God has given us and pursuing them with knowledge and skill. This knowledge comes by seeking the way of the kingdom first. We are learning to reign with Him. We are learning how to sit in heavenly places.

But there still are lessons to be learned in bodily death. The hardest lesson to be learned is that there are some things out of our control, and we must commit these things to the Lord.

Ironically, the ways of the kingdom compel an action-oriented life that equips us to rule and reign with Him in this life and in the life to come. We live active lives, implementing His *Crazy Kingdom*. We are continually learning a faith that believes and acts and affects this world instead of the world affecting us. Yet there is still a poignant lesson to be learned. There are still some things out of our control. Jesus, our perfect example of *Crazy Kingdom* living, shouts on the cross, "Into your hands I commit my spirit" (Luke 23:46). When Jesus did everything that was in His control and there was absolutely nothing more He could do, He

---

23. See 1 Corinthians 15:37-44.

committed His sacrifice to the Father. This is not faith. Faith acts. This is not vision. Vision sees and pursues. This is trust. *The committal of the body in death is the ultimate exercise in trust.*

This is true for our life, but it is also true for the ones we love. On October 8, 2010, my pregnant wife, daughter, and I were returning home from a vacation in Daytona Beach. We were hit by a teenager, and our precious four-year-old daughter was killed. He was initially charged with vehicular homicide DUI for driving under the influence of marijuana. A child's death is one of the most horrific situations any parent can go through, but it felt doubly depressing due to the fact we had been training her in *Crazy Kingdom* living. We had poured into her and prayed over her. God's miracle child to us was, for all practical purposes, gone.

We still don't understand why this happened. Why didn't God protect her? Why didn't He answer our prayers for her safety, her ministry, her husband, her career, our grandchildren? All we understood was that she was gone and the hopes we had for her had vanished as well. It was out of our control. We could not pray, act, or believe for anything. There was nothing we could do. After the long grieving process that we embraced, the only thing we could do was commit her to the Lord. We trust in Him, reminding ourselves, "There is a resurrection." Her dead body is not going to lay there lifeless in the grave forever. One day she will rise. She will have a bodily resurrection.

Jesus is the first fruits from the grave. When Jesus rose from the grave, He conquered death for all of His disciples. The power of life in the *Crazy Kingdom* is so much more powerful than death that even death bows fearfully in subjection to this radiating life.

The absolute deathblow to the survivalist mindset was delivered by Jesus. Jesus conquered death, and because He shares His victory with us, we have conquered death with Him. The liberation that Jesus brings us by breaking the grip of death opens the possibilities of this life. The survivalist mentality is cast out. Fear has been trampled. The resurrection power of Jesus and the *Crazy Kingdom* bring such a fearless life that we start living now instead of just existing. The *Crazy Kingdom* pushes one to live a robust life on the edge. We are able to push the limits of life to a place where a survivalist mindset doesn't fuel the fear of death. The *Crazy Kingdom* says, "Live fearlessly," and, "So what if you die?" Even if we die, we still live.

In light of this fearless existence, we can commit our lives and our loved ones to Him because He is the resurrection and the life. We have no idea which things His resurrection power is going to touch in the age to come. We are unaware of the dreams that will be resurrected. We don't comprehend what old hope will receive the breath of life or what relationship will be restored. We are blind to the moments that will be redeemed from this life. Moments stolen from us in the death of a loved one, in Him, will be returned. Redeemed and resurrected moments lost due to sin, sickness, unforgiveness, frailty, misunderstanding, and fear can all be resurrected. All we know is that if something is dead, then we have the opportunity to commit it to the hands of the One who is resurrection power.

As we wrap up this journey together, don't survive, but live life to the fullest. Don't live with small goals in security and safety, but live in such a robust way that it's dangerous. Then when you are birthed into heaven through the portals of death, tell the Lord, "Thank You for my life on earth. I turned it into an incredible adventure, and I can't wait to start my adventure here." And you will hear, "Well done, my good servant! …Because you have been trustworthy in a very small matter, take charge of ten cities" (Luke 19:17).

Business Application

Write out how your business/vocation can be used to create spiritual momentum moving into the next life.

Family Application

Have a family meeting and discuss how you can collectively start building spiritual momentum. Write out a game plan and work it out together.

Personal Application

Journal about the areas in which you want to build spiritual momentum for eternity.

Creative Application

Brainstorm all of the ways you can use your creative ability to carry momentum into eternity.

Solution Application

Of all of your solutions listed in this book, identify the top three that would have the greatest impact for eternity. How does this motivate you to solve problems?

Health Application

Write about how your physical health can help you build spiritual momentum.

Financial Application

How can you use your money to influence eternity? Write about it.

Prayer Application

Prayer has an incredible return. We will not know the full effect of our prayer until we are with Jesus. God answers every prayer—consider how powerful that is. It will be nothing less than amazing. Make sticky notes and put them around your house to encourage yourself to engage in prayer more often if that will help you. Purposefully and intentionally begin to apply prayer to every situation in your life.

CHAPTER 20

Conclusion

> The kingdom of heaven is like treasure hidden in a field. When a man found it, he hid it again, and then in his joy went and sold all he had and bought that field. (Matthew 13:44).

After the threat on my life in the parking lot, I quickly jumped in my truck and sped off to the nearest side street and cried. I decided to skip track practice that day and went home, where I called a friend who knew these guys. He informed me that I was dead. "These guys don't play," he told me. At that point he gave me the play-by-play of students they had harassed, beaten, or almost killed, and how they had covered their tracks. They hadn't actually killed anybody yet, but they were on the verge.

My friend was a new believer, and we went to the same youth group on Wednesday nights. I decided to ride with him that night because I was too upset to drive.

When the service began, the Lord began to speak to me from the start. The 300-plus-pound youth pastor had an unusual ritual during the youth service. He would go to the middle of the room, which was packed with over a hundred students. He would close his eyes and spin in a circle, and whoever he was pointing to when he stopped would have to read a Scripture. This night he pointed to a frightened sixth-grade girl who initially refused to read a Scripture, but with some persuasion flipped open her Bible, pointed to Deuteronomy 28:7, and began to read.

Crazy Kingdom

I was distracted until this point, but God had my laser focus from the moment she read, "The Lord will grant that the enemies who rise up against you will be defeated before you. They will come at you from one direction but flee from you in seven." My friend and I just looked at each other amazed.

But God was not finished speaking yet. During the worship time, the student-led band played the following songs: "The Battle Belongs To The Lord," "For the Lord is My Tower," and "Like Eagles," all of which speak of God's protection. Then the British youth pastor preached on God's ability to protect you as you make a stand for Christ. When the service ended, I knew God was going to keep me safe.

The next morning when I arrived at school, two friends were waiting for me. One friend was a strong believer who had unusual favor with the people in the drug culture. The other was a good friend who had gotten swept away by the tidal wave of drugs that hit our high school my sophomore year, but we still remained close. They began to walk with me down the long breezeway to the school's entrance and said, "Cameron, what have you done? Everyone we know is talking about killing you! These people are making real plans to hurt you!" I asked them to put in a good word for me and to try to talk people out of hurting me. They agreed to run interference for me, and the school day began.

This turned out to be a special day at school. We were having an assembly led by an evangelist from a local church. As I was getting ready to walk into the assembly, a group of the guys who had confronted me the day before were huddled up talking nearby. They were not the ringleaders, but they were a part of the group.

As this point I decided to just join the huddle. I was a teen before school shootings were a reality, so there was no danger in talking with them with teachers all around us. When I stepped in the huddle I said, "Hey guys, do you still have a problem with me?" They responded, "You better quit talking about our friend and you better quit preaching!"

Conclusion

I told them I would quit talking about their friend, but I would never stop preaching. They grudgingly consented, and I was feeling pretty good about how this was turning in my favor.

As the assembly started we learned this evangelist was unique in that he was infected with AIDS; this diagnosis lead to his conversion. As he began to tell of the dangers of doing drugs, sharing needles, and having unprotected sex, the atmosphere in the room was a bit distracted, even though the topic was very somber. The story of his looming death resulting from a life of addiction and sex didn't appear to faze the crowd.

He was getting ready to conclude and give the plug for the youth rally the church would have that night. He was probably going to say something similar to: "Something changed my life and if you come to so-and-so church, then they will have free pizza and you can hear the rest of the story." But what actually happened was he said, "Something has changed my life," and then was interrupted by a student who was sitting with the Marilyn Manson crowd. He jumped to his feet and yelled out, "What changed your life?" The evangelist said, "Jesus changed my life!"

The crowd was not really happy with that answer—especially not the group that had threatened me just the day before. Somehow the evangelist made his way toward them and began to warn them that if they didn't reject a life of drug abuse, then he feared their lives would be cut short.

In the weeks immediately following that confrontation, the five major leaders of our high school drug ring were displaced. Two were arrested on serious drug charges, and sadly, two were killed in a car accident while driving under the influence. The main ringleader was seriously injured from a fight in a bar that he illegally gained access to via a fake ID. This storm, the first of many, had passed; but I now realized I would be warding off my survival instinct for the rest of my life.

Closing Challenges

I want to challenge you to actually make intentional steps toward implementing the *Crazy Kingdom* principles listed in this book.

Face Your Fear!

Many people don't change or grow because they fear what change might mean for their comfort level, relationships, careers, etc. Many people feel the process of change would cause too many unnecessary problems. I challenge you to face your fears and fully understand that positive life change may cause a short-term upheaval in your life that could potentially create dozens of problems on many fronts. Be mentally prepared. You must pay the price others are not willing to pay. I challenge you to be resolved and to face your fears.

Stay Motivated!

Do you need to meet with a small group? Do you need an accountability partner? Do you need to intertwine these concepts within your daily devotions? Do you need to hire a life coach? Do you need to teach this book in your small group or Sunday school class? I want to challenge you to do whatever it takes to keep yourself motivated during the process of change. Learning and implementing any new life skill will have a learning curve attached to it. Enter the process of change. Know there will be moments of discouragement, but be prepared to have a support system in place to keep you motivated when you're down.

Embrace the Process!

How will you flesh out these changes? How will you carry out this process while ensuring the highest-quality results? I just told you that this process can cause a massive upheaval in every aspect of your life, but this doesn't give you a pass to be sloppy, unthoughtful, and reckless in your efforts for change. You'll face enough problems when you implement these principles with wisdom. You wouldn't want to compound your troubles through careless implementation. I want to

Conclusion

challenge you to get out your journal and your calendar and develop a plan for slow, steady, and incremental change. Form a game plan. Set dates and deadlines. Think through how this might influence your spouse, children, employees, bosses, and friends. Make small and thoughtful adjustments, remembering to be considerate of others. An intentional and personalized strategy that considers one's own context will ensure success. Making changes as gracefully as possible will increase your influence with others and will draw them into the path of *Crazy Kingdom* living much more quickly.

Be Thorough!

Work the *Crazy Kingdom* into every nook and cranny of your life. Jesus said, "The kingdom of heaven is like yeast that a woman took and mixed into about sixty pounds of flour until it worked all through the dough." The kingdom must be worked throughout the whole batch of dough. The dough is your life and everything your life has influence over or within. If you're diligent, the yeast will spread and change the very essence of your life and dominion.

Thank you for choosing a path that is so much the opposite of the course of this world. Your diligent efforts will transform your very life and everything you touch. You'll bring heaven to your domain. Your satisfaction will be great, your reward even greater. Finally, remember this: never allow anyone to ever persuade you to leave the *Crazy Kingdom*. Be resolved and determined. May the Lord bless you in your efforts as you thrive in the inside-out and upside-down, but truly right-side up, *Crazy Kingdom*.

About the Author

Cameron King is the lead pastor of NewSong Church, where he has served as pastor since 2013. Cameron has a knack for taking troubled churches and transforming them into healthy communities of faith. Cameron activates Christians into the supernatural gifts of the Spirit and trains them how to hear from God. His personal mission is to help serious disciples develop intimacy with God, move in power, and live principle-centered lives. His blog and website RoyalPerspectives.com is dedicated to this end. He is also the author of *The Key to Your Church's Vision: the Practical Guide to Praying for Your Pastor.*

Cameron has been married to his wife, Rachel, since 2002. Cameron and Rachel have also started Royal Remnant Properties which is a for profit business that provides high quality and safe rental houses for low income people. They live in the Atlanta metro area with their four daughters, Abigail, Alena, Maddie Grace, and Eliana.

Cameron can be contacted at johncameronking@yahoo.com.

www.ingramcontent.com/pod-product-compliance
Lightning Source LLC
Chambersburg PA
CBHW051950290426
44110CB00015B/2183